THE SOUTH DOWNS WAY NOTE BOOK

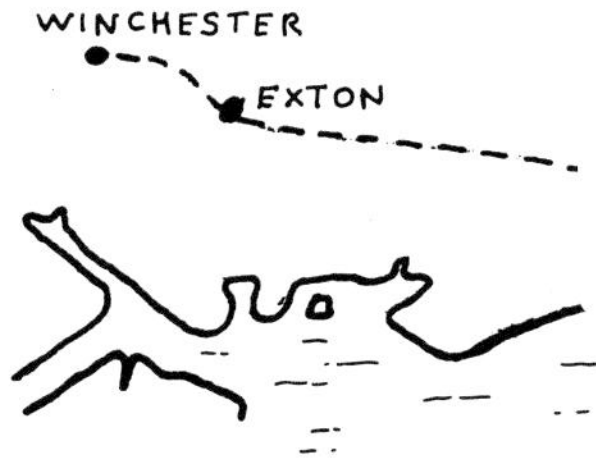

CONTENTS

INTRODUCTION

WHY WALK THE SOUTH DOWNS WAY?
THE PLEASURE AND BEAUTY OF THE COUNTRYSIDE,
THE CHALLENGE OF A LONG DISTANCE EXPEDITION.
IT IS YOUR RIGHT TO NAVIGATE, WITHOUT TRESPASS THE PATHS OF THIS COUNTRY

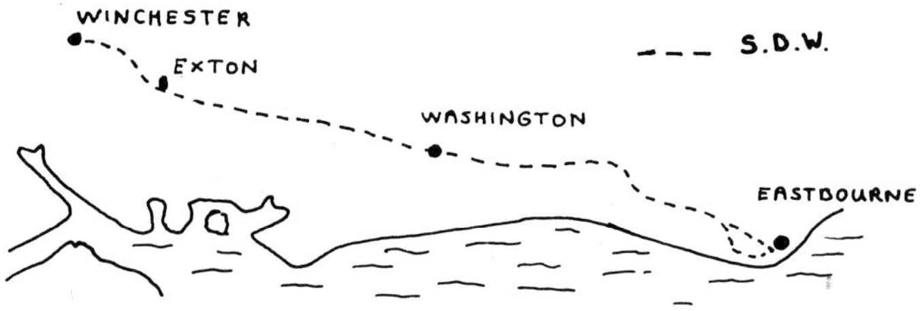

WHATEVER THE REASON THE SOUTH DOWNS WAY CATERS FOR MANY LIKES IN ITS 100 MILE (160 km) JOURNEY THROUGH TWO COUNTIES.
FROM ANCIENT CITIES AND RURAL VILLAGES TO ROLLING DOWNLAND AND SPECTACULAR COAST.
HISTORY, GEOGRAPHY, AND GEOLOGY ARE THERE FOR THE OBSERVANT AND INTERESTED.
PLANTS, BIRDS AND OTHER ANIMAL LIFE ARE THERE FOR THE QUIET AND PATIENT.
AGRICULTURE, WITH ITS SOCIAL AND ECONOMIC DEVELOPMENT CAN BE WITNESSED BY THE SLOW THOUGHTFUL TRAVELLER.
THE SOUTH DOWNS WAY IS A PRODUCT OF THE COUNTRYSIDE COMMISSION WHO IN 1972 OPENED THE BURITON TO EASTBOURNE SECTION AND THEN THE WINCHESTER EXTENSION IN 1989.
ALL OF THE SOUTH DOWNS WAY PASSES THROUGH AREAS OF OUTSTANDING NATURAL BEAUTY, AND THE SEVEN SISTERS COUNTRY PARK IS CLASSIFIED AS HERITAGE COAST.

WHY TRAVEL FROM WEST TO EAST?

ANSWERED FROM A LOGISTICAL POINT OF VIEW, A BOOK IS READ FROM FRONT TO BACK, AND EACH PAGE LEFT TO RIGHT.
THIS TRANSLATES VERY NATURALLY TO WEST TO EAST MAPPING AND WALKING.
A GEOGRAPHICAL EXPLANATION OF WEST TO EAST IS SOMEWHAT SIMPLER:
AS THE WALKER WILL TELL YOU THE FINAL DESCENT IN TO EASTBOURNE IS JUST THAT, THE FINAL DESCENT. THERE ARE NO MORE HILLS TO WALK AND HENCE AN OBVIOUS CONCLUSION TO A DOWNLAND WALK.
WINCHESTER CONVERSELY IS A ROUTE CENTRE, WITH ROADS, RAIL, FOOTPATHS AND RIVERS GOING IN MANY DIRECTIONS AND, MORE IMPORTANTLY, NO OBVIOUS SATISFACTORY END TO THE SOUTH DOWNS WAY.
THE START, OR FINISH BOARD, WHICHEVER WAY YOU WISH TO VIEW IT, AT WINCHESTER, IS BESIDE THE M3 MOTORWAY.
IT IS FOR THIS REASON THAT WE HAVE TAKEN A DEGREE OF ARTISTIC LICENCE AND STARTED THE WALKING INSTRUCTIONS AT KING ALFREDS STATUE.
THIS HAS THE ADVANTAGE THAT THE STATUE IS EASY TO FIND, AND WHAT GRANDER START TO THE WALK THAN THE FIRST STEP WALKING IN THE SHADOW OF A KING.

USING THE GUIDE

THIS GUIDE IS DIVIDED INTO 9 SECTIONS REPRESENTING A SUGGESTED DAYS WALKING.
AT THE BEGINNING OF EACH SECTION IS A ONE PAGE INTRODUCTION GIVING A BRIEF OUTLINE OF THE FORTHCOMING ROUTE.
THE FOLLOWING PAGES CONTAIN A DETAILED MAP AND WALKING INSTRUCTIONS, WITH DRAWINGS AND TEXT.

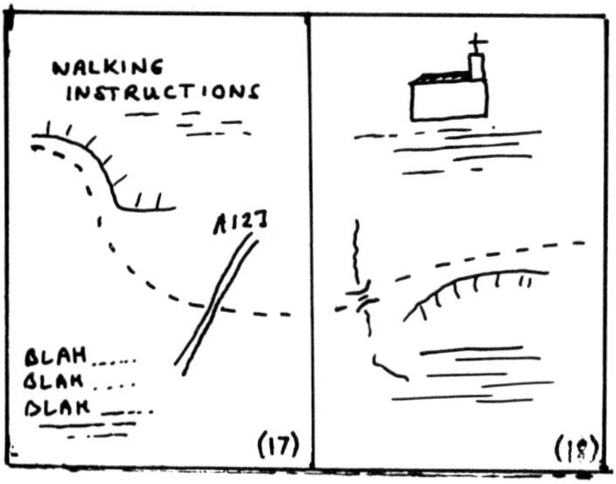

MAPS

ARE OF A CONTINUOUS STRIP FORMAT, AND ARE DRAWN TO SCALE OF 4cm TO 1Km OR 2½ INCHES TO 1 MILE, WITH AS MANY LOCALISED AND RELEVANT FEATURES DRAWN IN AS POSSIBLE.
MAPS BY ORDNANCE SURVEY AND HARVEY MAPS COVER THE ROUTE, AND IT IS ADVISED THAT THEY BE USED IN CONJUNCTION WITH THE GUIDE TO OBTAIN AN OVERALL PICTURE OF DISTANCE AND RELIEF.

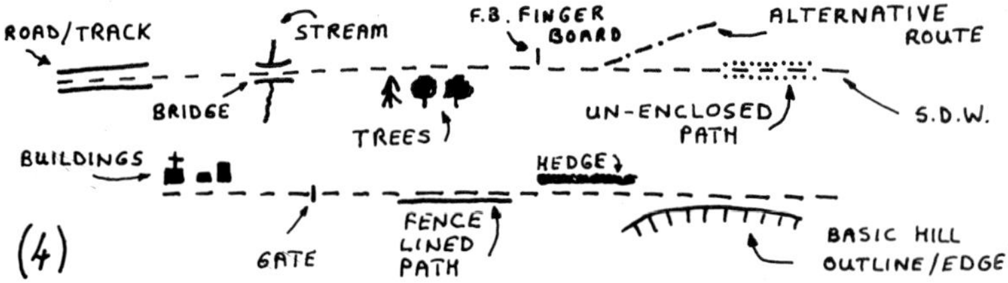

PRINCIPAL ROADS, PLACES AND RIVERS ALONG THE SOUTH DOWNS WAY.

W	WINCHESTER
E	EXTON
B	BURITON
C	COCKING
A	AMBERLEY
WA	WASHINGTON
P	PYECOMBE
S	SOUTHEASE
AL	ALFRISTON
EB	EASTBOURNE

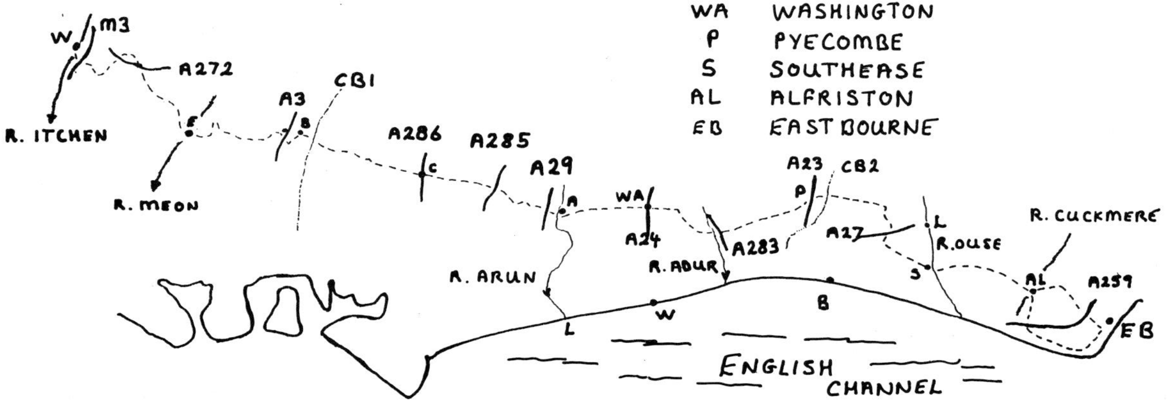

C.B1 COUNTY BOUNDARY HAMPSHIRE / SUSSEX

CB2 COUNTY BOUNDARY W. SUSSEX / E. SUSSEX

COASTAL TOWNS

B	BRIGHTON
W	WORTHING
L	LITTLEHAMPTON

THE FORMATION OF THE DOWNS / GEOLOGY

TO THE INTERESTED EYE IT WILL NOT TAKE LONG BEFOR OBSERVATION QUESTIONS RELATING TO THE SHAPE OF THE LAND BEGIN TO EMERGE.
WHY DOES THAT U SHAPED VALLEY SNAKE ITS WAY AROUND THE HILLS?
WHY IS THE SLOPE OF THE DOWNS GENTLE TO THE SOUT AND STEEP TO THE NORTH?
WHY ARE THE DOWNS CHALKY GRASSLAND AND YET AT THE BASE OF EACH HILL IT IS MUDDY CLAY?

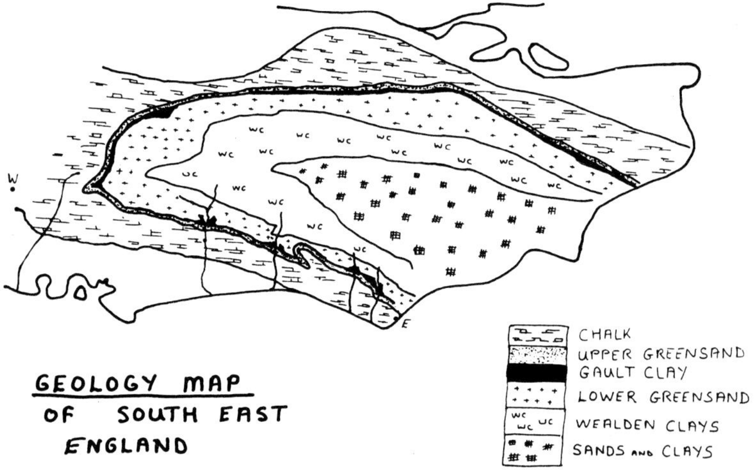

GEOLOGY MAP
OF SOUTH EAST ENGLAND

THE SIMPLE ANSWER IS THAT THE LANDSCAPE WE SEE IS THE PRODUCT OF THE LAST ICE AGE.
THE VAST ICE SHEETS OF 10,000 YEARS AGO, GOUGED, SCRAPED, FROZE, THAWED, CRACKED, DISSOLVED AND FLOODED THE SOFT CHALK.
THE FINAL SHAPING, REMEMBERING THAT THIS IS AN ON-GOING PROCESS, IS THE PRODUCT OF THE MANY STREAMS AND RIVERS THAT CROSS THE LANDSCAPE, AND OF COURSE THE INFLUENCE OF MAN.

THE SOUTH DOWNS FORMATION... A LITTLE MORE IN DEPTH.

PPROXIMATELY 100 MILLION YEARS AGO (MA) THE SOUTH F ENGLAND WAS A SWAMP, WHERE RIVERS DEPOSITED ANDS AND CLAYS.

S THE YEARS PASSED THE SEA BEGAN TO INVADE THE

AND AND PRODUCED A SERIES OF SAND AND CLAY, IN .AYERS : THE LOWER GREENSAND, GAULT CLAY, AND THE UPPER GREENSAND.

MORE YEARS PASSED AND THE SEA LEVELS ROSE STILL IIGHER, ALLOWING A "CHALK SEA" TO FLOURISH.

CHALK SEA IS SO NAMED BECAUSE SEA CREATURES CALLED COCCOLITHS LIVE IN THE SEA, AND UPON THEIR DEATH SINK TO THE BOTTOM, COMPRESS AND FORM CHALK.

OVER THE 40 MA* THAT THIS PROCESS WENT ON FOR, DEPTH OF CHALK IN THE ORDER OF 1000 METRES THICK BUILT UP.

THE SEA LEVELS THEN FELL AND THIS VAST EXPANSE OF CHALK WAS SUBJECT TO BUCKLING INTO A DOME SHAPE BY THE ALPINE OROGENY.... A RESULT OF AFRICA COLLIDING WITH EUROPE.

HE ICE AGES THEN ERODED THE DOME, AND CLEARED HE WEALD LEAVING THE SHAPES THAT WE SEE ON THE DOWNS, AND THE EXTENSIVE VIEWS OVER THE WEALD.

T IS A POWERFUL THOUGHT THAT THE S. DOWNS BEFORE THE ICE WERE THE HEIGHT OF BEN NEVIS NOW, AND THAT THE SEA LEVEL AT THE TIME OF THE CHALK SEA WAS 500 METRES HIGHER THAN IT IS NOW.

*MA: MILLION YEARS

Winchester City Centre

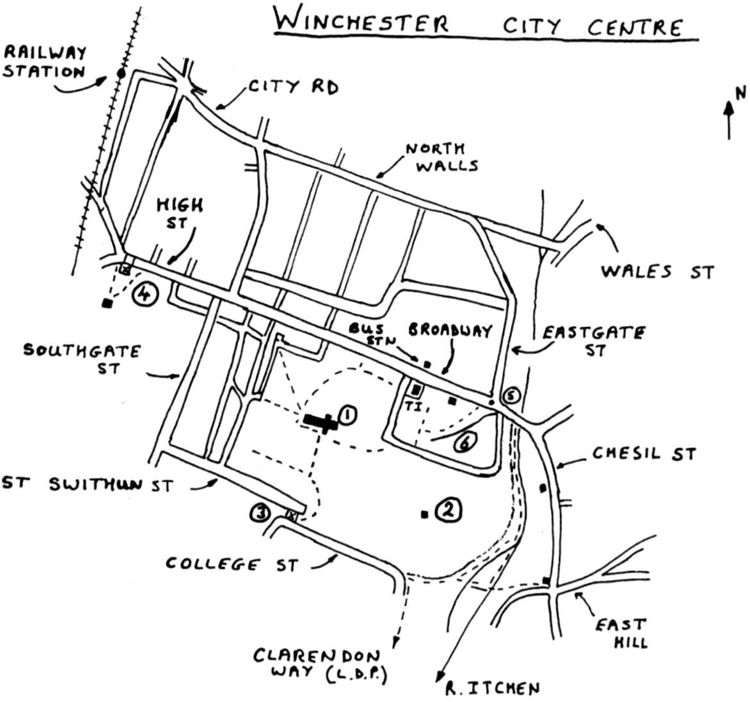

① CATHEDRAL
② WOLVESEY CASTLE / PALACE
③ KINGSGATE
④ WESTGATE, MUSEUM, CASTLE REMAINS, LAW COURTS
⑤ KING ALFRED'S STATUE
⑥ ABBEY GARDENS

---- FOOTPATHS

WINCHESTER

HAS HAD ITS PLACE IN THE HISTORY BOOKS FOR MANY YEARS NOW: SOCIAL, RELIGIOUS, MILITARY... INDEED TOUCHED BY ALL OF THE MANY INFLUENCES THAT GO TO MAKE UP THE DEVELOPMENT OF AN AREA.

THE KNOWN HISTORY DATES TO 450 BC WHERE THERE IS EVIDENCE OF A SETTLEMENT ON, WHAT IS NOW, ST CATHERINES HILL.

IN THE 2500 YEARS SINCE:

THE ROMANS (50 TO 400 AD) CAME AND LEFT.

THE DARK AGES (400 TO 600) AND THE SUGGESTION THAT WINCHESTER MAY HAVE BEEN KING ARTHUR'S CAMELOT.

THE SAXON PERIOD SAW WINCHESTER BECOME A ROYAL AND HOLY CITY, AND IN THE LATE ⓒ9 WAS KING ALFRED'S AND ENGLAND'S CAPITAL.

THE NORMAN CONQUEST IN 1066 SAW THE BUILDING OF THE WOLVESEY CASTLE AND PALACE AND IN 1079 THE PRESENT CATHEDRAL WAS STARTED.

IN THE LAST 1000 YEARS WINCHESTER HAS BORNE WITNESS TO SOCIAL EVENTS SUCH AS THE DOMESDAY BOOK IN 1086, THE BLACK DEATH IN 1348, HENRY VIII ENTERTAINING IN THE GREAT HALL IN 1520 AND DESTROYING THE SAINT SWITHUN SHRINE, AS PART OF THE DISSOLUTION OF THE MONASTERIES, IN 1538.

COMMUNICATIONS HAVE LARGELY BEEN THE PRODUCT OF THE LAST TWO CENTURIES AS A RESULT OF THE CONSTRUCTION OF THE RAILWAY IN 1840.

THE ⓒ20 SAW THE GROWTH OF ROAD TRANSPORT, SPECIFICALLY THE NEW BY PASS IN 1937, SUBSEQUENTLY REPLACED BY THE M3 MOTORWAY IN 1994.

WINCHESTER.

AT THE WESTERN END OF THE HIGH STREET IS THE WESTGATE.

THIS MEDIEVAL GATEWAY AND THE SURROUNDING CASTLE REMAINS MAKES FOR AN EXCELLENT ENTRANCE TO THE HIGH ST AND CITY.

WINCHESTER IS A VERY PEDESTRIAN FRIENDLY CITY. A NUMBER OF ROADS HAVE BEEN RE-ROUTED, AND THE HIGH STREET IS A PAVED PRECINCT, TO THE EXTENT THAT WALKING IS BY FAR THE EASIEST METHOD OF SEEING THE CITY, AND THE MOST INFORMATIVE, SINCE WALLS AND MONUMENTS ARE ADORNED WITH INFORMATION.

EVERY SIDE ROAD, ALLEY AND COURTYARD PRODUCES YET ANOTHER PICTURE OF THE HISTORY OF WINCHESTER, ALONG WITH SOME IDYLLIC PLACES TO SIT AND MULL OVER ONE'S NEW FOUND KNOWLEDGE.

AN AFTERNOON IN WINCHESTER IS AN AFTERNOON WELL SPENT.

WINCHESTER

THE CATHEDRAL

TWO CLASSIC VIEWS OF THE 900 YEAR OLD CATHEDRAL

A NUMBER OF PATHS AND COURTYARDS RING THE AREA SURROUNDING THE CATHEDRAL AND WOLVESEY PALACE AND CASTLE.

WINCHESTER

WHILST TRYING TO COVER ALL THE ASPECTS OF WINCHESTER'S HISTORY IN A VOLUME SUCH AS THIS WOULD BE UNWISE AND UNNECESSARY, ONE STORY IS PERHAPS RATHER APPROPRIATE TO RELATE.

THE SAINT SWITHUN STORY

SAINT SWITHUN WAS THE BISHOP OF WINCHESTER WHO, UPON HIS DEATH IN 862, REQUESTED HE BE BURIED BESIDE THE WEST DOOR OF THE MINSTER. SOME 109 YEARS LATER IN 971 THE THEN BISHOP AETHELWOLD ORDERED THAT THE GRAVE BE OPENED, AS PART OF BUILDING WORKS, AND RE-BURIED IN THE THEN NEW MINSTER, NOW KNOWN AS THE OLD MINSTER.

AS A RESULT OF RAIN ON THAT FATEFUL DAY THE LEGEND OF 40 DAYS OF RAIN WAS BORNE.

SO IF IT IS ANYWHERE NEAR THE 15TH JULY, AND IT RAINS WE DO HOPE YOU HAVE YOUR WATERPROOFS WITH YOU.

FOR PERSONS OF A MORE SCIENTIFIC LEANING AN EXCELLENT WEATHER STATION CAN BE FOUND ON THE WALL VERY CLOSE TO KING ALFRED'S STATUE.

SAINT WHO?

WINCHESTER

KING ALFRED'S STATUE CAN BE FOUND AT THE EASTERN END OF THE BROADWAY, AND STANDS AS A MONUMENT TO THE SAXON KING WHO MADE WINCHESTER THIS COUNTRY'S CAPITAL CITY.

FROM A PRACTICAL VIEW POINT, WE HAVE EXERCISED A LITTLE ARTISTIC LICENCE AND STARTED THE SOUTH DOWNS WAY WALKING INSTRUCTIONS FROM THE STATUE. IT WILL BECOME OBVIOUS WHY WHEN THE OFFICIAL START BOARD IS MET.

THE FOOTPATH, ON THE WEST SIDE OF THE RIVER, OFFERS A VERY PEACEFUL EXIT FROM WINCHESTER TO THE S.D.W.

CITY BRIDGE AND THE C18 MILL. (NOW A YOUTH HOSTEL)

TURN LEFT AND UP WHARF HILL TO THE KINGS HEAD P.H.

WINCHESTER TO EXTON 12m 19km

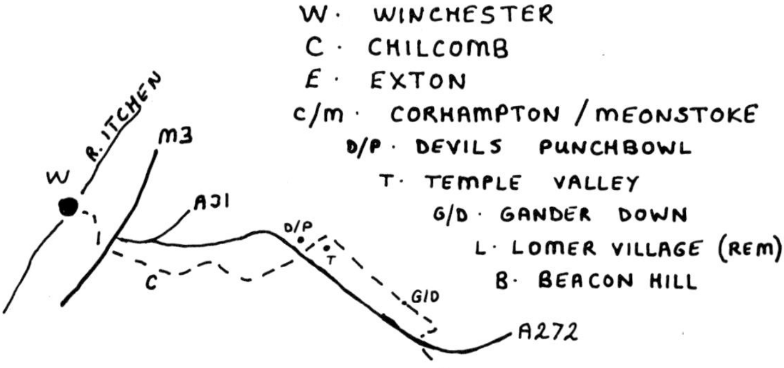

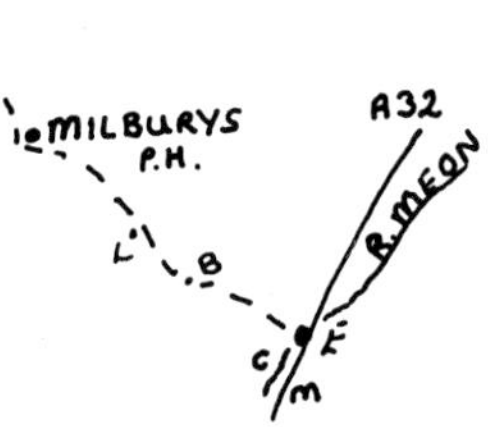

THIS SECTION IS AN EASY GOING INTRODUCTION TO THE S.D.W, BUT NEVERTHELESS OFFERING A GOOD SELECTION OF THE DELIGHTS THAT BECOME OLD FRIENDS AS THE MILES PROGRESS.

FROM THE LOVELY OLD CITY OF WINCHESTER AND THE GHASTLY NOISE OF THE M3, THE PATH QUICKLY ENTERS THE PEACEFUL WORLDS OF CHILCOMB VILLAGE, FAWLEY DOWN, TEMPLE VALLEY AND THE FIRST SIGNS OF ANCIENT LIFE ON GANDER DOWN.

A SECOND BRIEF FLIRTATION WITH THE A272, AND THE PATH PASSES THE MILBURYS P.H, WIND FARM, AND LOMER FARM, WHERE THE WAYFARERS WALK CROSSES THE S.D.W, AND THE REMAINS OF LOMER VILLAGE CAN BE FOUND.

THE BEAUTIFUL BEECH TREES OF BEACON HILL, WITH A GLIMPSE OF SOUTHAMPTON AND THE ISLE OF WIGHT TO THE S.W. ARE THE FINAL VIEWS OF THE DAY BEFORE THE DESCENT TO EXTON AND THE MEON VALLEY.

WINCHESTER TO EXTON

ROM KING ALFRED'S STATUE GO EAST ALONG BRIDGE ST
ND CROSS THE BRIDGE.
URN RIGHT AT THE ROUNDABOUT IN TO CHESIL ST AND
OLLOW TO THE KINGS HEAD P.H.
URN LEFT IN TO EASTHILL AND CONTINUE, BEARING TO
HE RIGHT, IN TO PETERSFIELD RD.
TAY WITH THE PETERSFIELD RD UNTIL IT TURNS LEFT
TO CHALK RIDGE, WHERE THE S.D.W. CONTINUES ON THE
PATH TO THE
OFFICIAL START

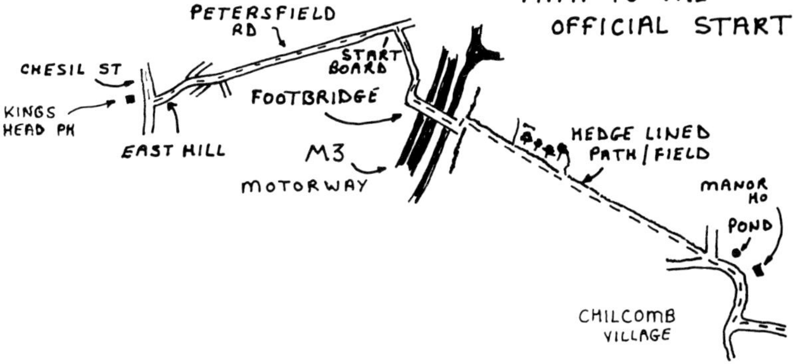

FOLLOW THE WAYMARKER ARROWS TO THE RIGHT
ND THEN AROUND TO THE LEFT OVER THE M3 FOOTBRIDGE
URN LEFT AND THEN
IGHT, TO CROSS THE
IELD, BESIDE THE
EDGE LINE.
OLLOW THE ROAD
HROUGH THE
ILLAGE OF
HILCOMB

THE OFFICIAL
SOUTH DOWNS WAY START BOARD.

THE SOUTH DOWNS WAY .... WAYMARKERS.

THE NATIONAL TRAIL ACORN

STONE MARKERS

YELLOW ARROW : FOOTPATH ONLY
BLUE ARROW : BRIDLEWAY
(HORSES, BICYCLES, WALKERS)

THE TRADITIONAL FINGER BOARD

ONTINUE ON THE TARMAC ROAD THROUGH CHILCOMB AND
N TO THE DOWNS, WHERE A LEFT TURN CONTINUES THE
LIMB ON A HEDGE LINED TRACK.

LTERNATIVE ROUTE:

TREE LINED PATH CAN BE FOUND JUST IN TO THE TREE-
NE BEYOND A HOUSE CALLED HILLACRE WHICH RE-JOINS
IE S.D.W. AT THE JUNCTION WITH GIPSY LANE.

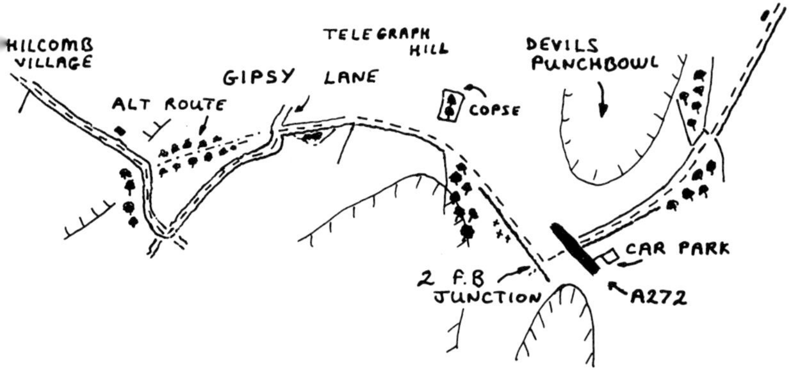

FOLLOW THE TRACK ON TO TELEGRAPH HILL, AND ON TO THE TWO FINGER BOARD JUNCTION, WHERE A LEFT TURN CROSSES THE FIELD AND A272.
CONTINUE AHEAD ALONG THE PATH.

HE TWO FINGER BOARD JUNCTION
BESIDE THE A272.

HE VIEW TO THE LEFT (WEST) IS THE DEVILS PUNCHBOWL,
ND JUST BEYOND THE TREES ON THE RIGHT (EAST)
S TEMPLE VALLEY.

THE DEVILS PUNCHBOWL

THE FIRST OF MANY DEVILISH NAMES FOR SPECTACULAR NATURAL FEATURES, TO BE FOUND ALONG THE SOUTH DOWNS WAY.
THE DEVILS PUNCHBOWL IS A GLACIAL VALLEY, AS THE DISTINCTIVE U SHAPE CLEARLY SHOWS.
IN APRIL 1944, PRIOR TO THE D. DAY LANDINGS, AMASSING ALLIED TROOPS STAGED A BOXING TOURNAMENT IN THE PUNCHBOWL FEATURING THE THEN HEAVY WEIGHT CHAMPION JOE LOUIS.
THE CHALK SLOPES ARE ALSO HOME TO RARE, ALTHOUGH INDIGENOUS, PLANTS SUCH AS FROG ORCHID AND CUSTARD BELLFLOWER.

CONTINUE ON THE FOOTPATH THROUGH THE TWO COPSE OF TREES UNTIL THE FARM BUILDINGS.

TURN RIGHT ON TO THE HEDGE LINED TRACK AND CONTINUE OVER GANDER DOWN AND ON TO GANDERDOWN FARM.

CROSS THE FIELD USING THE TREE LINE AND POSTS. THE NEXT FIELD MUST BE FOLLOWED AROUD THE EDGE.

IF FENCE ON THE LEFT.

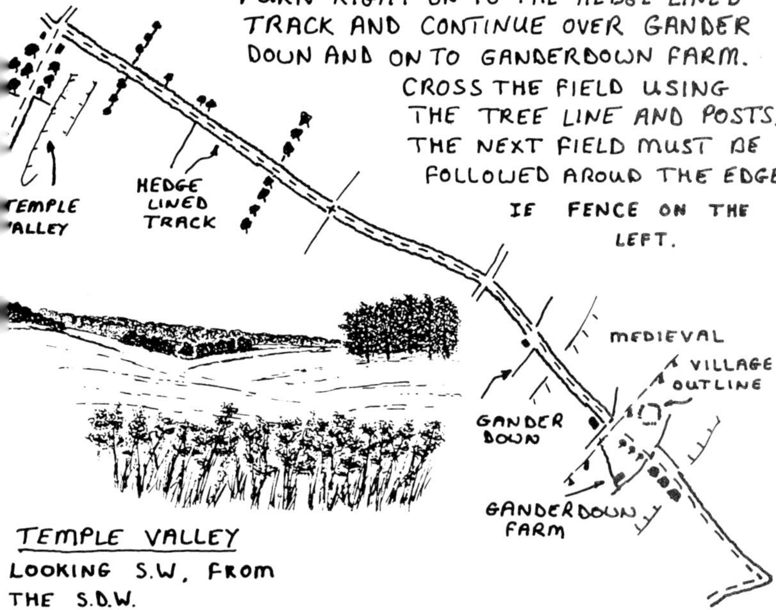

TEMPLE VALLEY

LOOKING S.W. FROM THE S.D.W.

APPROACHING GANDERDOWN FARM

THE SQUARE OUTLINE TO THE NORTH (LEFT) OF THE PATH, IS THE REMAINS OF A MEDIEVAL VILLAGE.

TURN LEFT, THROUGH THE GATE, TO THE ROAD (A272) WHICH IS CROSSED AND THE TREE LIN[ED] TRACK OPPOSITE. FOLLOW THROUGH HOLDEN FM. AND ALONG HOLDEN LANE TO THE JUNCTION AT WINDMILL FARM.

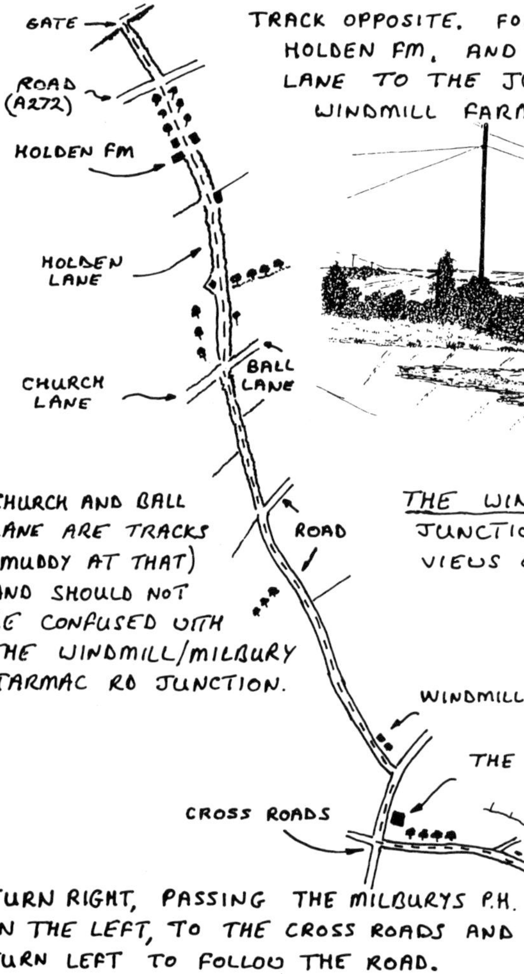

THE WINDMILL FARM JUNCTION..... GOOD VIEWS OF NORTH DOWNS.

CHURCH AND BALL LANE ARE TRACKS (MUDDY AT THAT) AND SHOULD NOT BE CONFUSED WITH THE WINDMILL/MILBURY TARMAC RD JUNCTION.

TURN RIGHT, PASSING THE MILBURYS P.H. ON THE LEFT, TO THE CROSS ROADS AND TURN LEFT TO FOLLOW THE ROAD.
FOR SAFETYS SAKE THE PATH IS TO THE SIDE OF THE ROAD, AND IF FOLLOWED THE CROSSING POINT TO WIND[MILL] FARM AND THE TRACK FOR LOMER FARM ARE EASILY FOUND

THE MILBURYS FREE HOUSE.

VERY CONVENIENTLY, THE S.D.W. PASSES THE MILBURYS P.H. JUST AS LUNCH IS BECKONING.

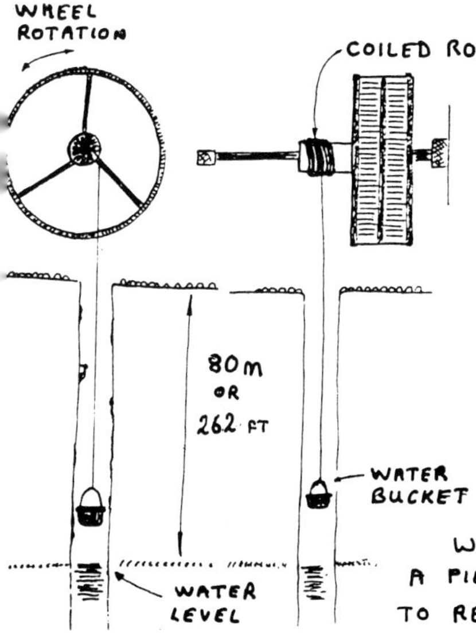

TO THE BACK OF THE PUB IS A 16TH CENTURY TREAD MILL. THE TREAD MILL WOULD HAVE BEEN ROTATED TO RAISE AND LOWER THE WATER BUCKET IN TO THE WELL. CHALK IS A POROUS ROCK, THAT WHEN DUG DOWN INTO THE WATER TABLE WILL EVENTUALLY BE FOUND. A PIECE OF ICE TOOK 8 SECS TO REACH THE WATER, AND

ROM THAT TIME WE WOULD SUGGEST A FALL OF 80m.

STAY ON THE TRACK TO AND THROUGH LOMER FARM, PAST THE REMAINS OF LOMER VILLAGE AND POND TO TH THE TARMAC RD WHICH IS FOLLOWED TO BEACON HILL BEECH. THE S.D.W. PATH CROSSES THE FIELD DIAGONALLY AND RE-JOINS THE ROAD.

TURN LEFT, AND FOLLOW THE ROAD TO A FINGER BOARD, WHERE A PATH IS FOLLOWED ACROSS THE FIELD AND DOWN THE HILL TOWARD THE TREE LINE.

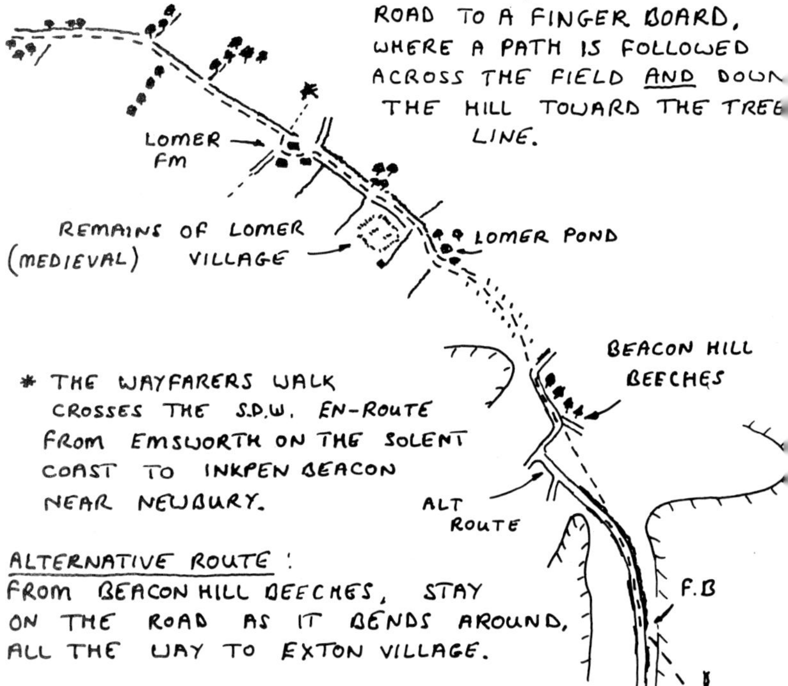

* THE WAYFARERS WALK CROSSES THE S.D.W. EN-ROUTE FROM EMSWORTH ON THE SOLENT COAST TO INKPEN BEACON NEAR NEWBURY.

ALTERNATIVE ROUTE:
FROM BEACON HILL BEECHES, STAY ON THE ROAD AS IT BENDS AROUND, ALL THE WAY TO EXTON VILLAGE.

BEACON HILL

THE PATH DESCENDS THE DOWN AND THEN CROSSES FOUR FIELDS DIAGONALLY, WITH A TRACK BETWEEN THE SECOND AND THIRD.

THE PATH EMERGES ON TO A SMALL TARMAC LANE.

TURN LEFT THROUGH THE VILLAGE, PASSING THE CHURCH AND MANOR FM TO THE ROAD

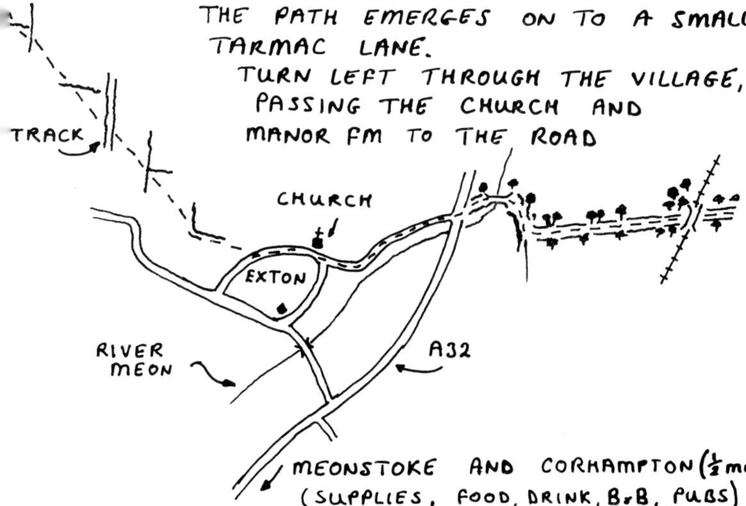

MEONSTOKE AND CORHAMPTON (½ MILE)
(SUPPLIES, FOOD, DRINK, B&B, PUBS)

EXTON CHURCH.
THE FIRST OF MANY TO BE VISITED ALONG THE SOUTH DOWNS WAY (S.D.W)

THE MEON VALLEY

THE RIVER MEON, A VERY PRETTY CHALK STREAM, FLOWS THROUGH THE VILLAGES OF EXTON, CORHAMPTON AND MEONSTOKE.

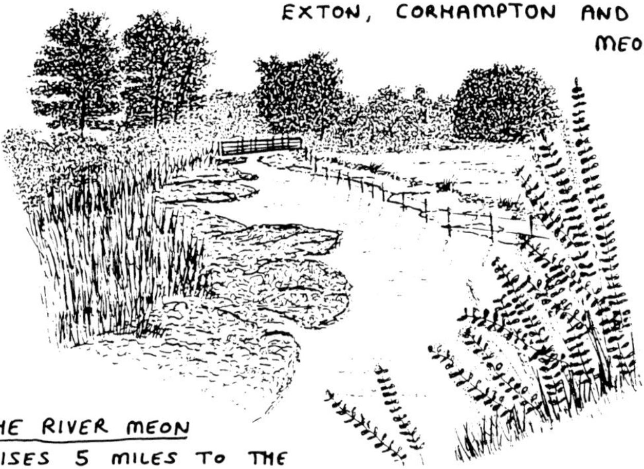

THE RIVER MEON

RISES 5 MILES TO THE EAST, NEAR THE VILLAGE OF EAST MEON, AND JOINS THE SOLENT 30 MILES TO THE SOUTH.

THE VILLAGES OF THE MEON VALLEY MAKE EXCELLENT STOPPING POINTS AT THE END OF THIS FIRST SECTION.

EXTON TO BURITON 12·5m 20km

E · EXTON
B · BURITON

T/H · TEGDOWN HILL
B/H · BUTSER HILL

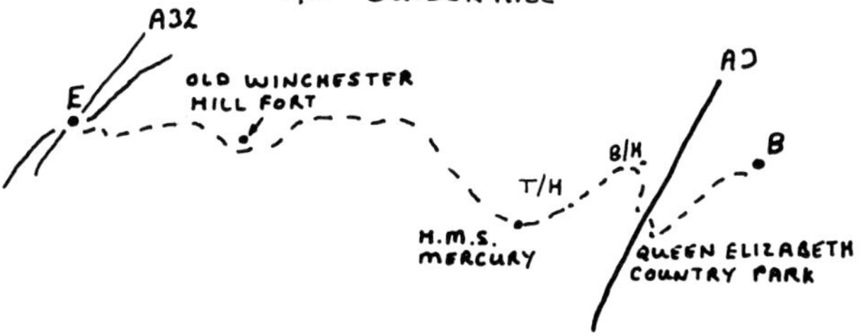

LEAVING THE MEON VALLEY BY THE SIDE OF THE CHALK STREAM AND BRIDGE IS A DELIGHT.
A CLOSED RAILWAY AND BRIDGE, AND THE CLIMB IS UNDERWAY TO THE TOP OF OLD WINCHESTER HILL, AND THE REMAINS OF THE IRON AGE FORT.
THE VIEWS ARE EXCELLENT AND WELL DOCUMENTED IF A LITTLE PATIENCE IS EXERCISED AT THE MAP TOP BOARD.
THE LONG GENTLE CLIMB ON TO SALTHILL PROVIDES EXCELLENT VIEWS ON THREE POINTS OF THE COMPASS.
FROM H.M.S. MERCURY THE WALK OVER HYDEN HILL, TEGDOWN HILL AND ON TO BUTSER HILL IS EASY WITH SPLENDID VIEWS OVER THE MEON VALLEY.
THE A3 MERCIFULLY, IS CROSSED BY AN UNDERPASS, AND IS FOLLOWED BY A DELIGHTFUL WALK THROUGH THE QUEEN ELIZABETH COUNTRY PARK.
THE FINAL VIEW OF THE DAY IS OF THE ROTHER VALLEY, PETERSFIELD AND BURITON.

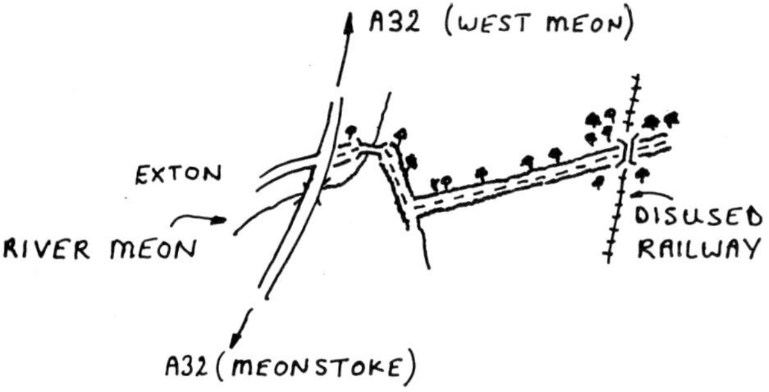

LEAVING EXTON, CROSS THE MAIN ROAD A32 AND PROCEED ALONG THE FOOTPATH OPPOSITE TO THE BRIDGE. CROSS THE BRIDGE AND CONTINUE TO A LEFT TURN IN TO A STRAIGHT, TREE AND HEDGE LINED PATH.

THE PATH IS DEEPLY RECESSED AND NEARLY ONE MILE IN LENGTH.

APPROXIMATELY HALF A MILE ALONG IS A RAIL BRIDGE AND THE DISUSED LINE.

IN DRY CONDITIONS THE PATH IS EASY,...

... BUT IN THE WET IT IS MUDDY AND OFTEN UNDERWATER NECESSITATING A SCRAMBLE ALONG THE EDGE.

BRIDGE OVER THE RIVER MEON.

UPON REACHING ROLLS COPSE, AND THE CONCRETE TRACK, TURN RIGHT AND THEN FOLLOW THE TRACK, ON THE LEFT OF THE TREE LINE.
STAY WITH THE FENCE AND HEDGE LINED TRACK, AND CLIMB OLD WINCHESTER HILL.
LEAVE THE HILL FORT VIA THE EASTERN RAMPARTS.

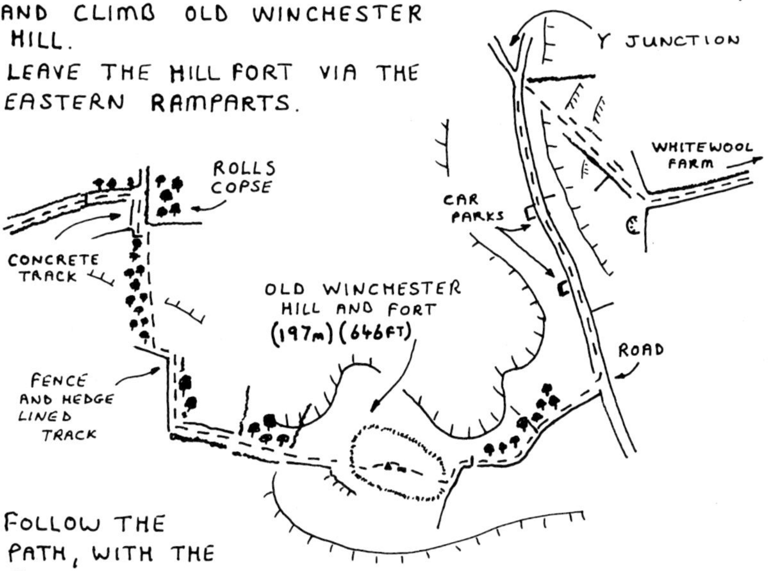

FOLLOW THE PATH, WITH THE FENCE ON YOUR RIGHT, AROUND TO THE ROAD.
FOLLOW THE ROAD TO A Y JUNCTION, WHERE THE PATH TURNS RIGHT AND DESCENDS STEEPLY A FIELD.
AT A GATE AND FENCE JUNCTION, TURN LEFT TO WHITEWOOL FARM.

OLD WINCHESTER HILL FROM ROLLS COPSE

OLD WINCHESTER HILL

APPROACHING THE
TRIG POINT AND MAP BOARD FROM THE WEST.

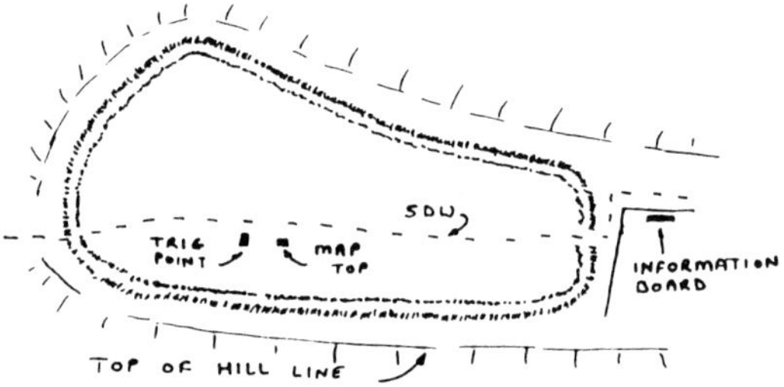

BASIC OUTLINE OF THE
IRON AGE HILL FORT.

INFORMATION
BOARD

EARTH RAMPARTS ON THE EASTERN
END OF THE HILL FORT.

FOLLOW THE DRIVE AROUND TO THE LEFT (NORTH) OF WHITEWOOL FARM.

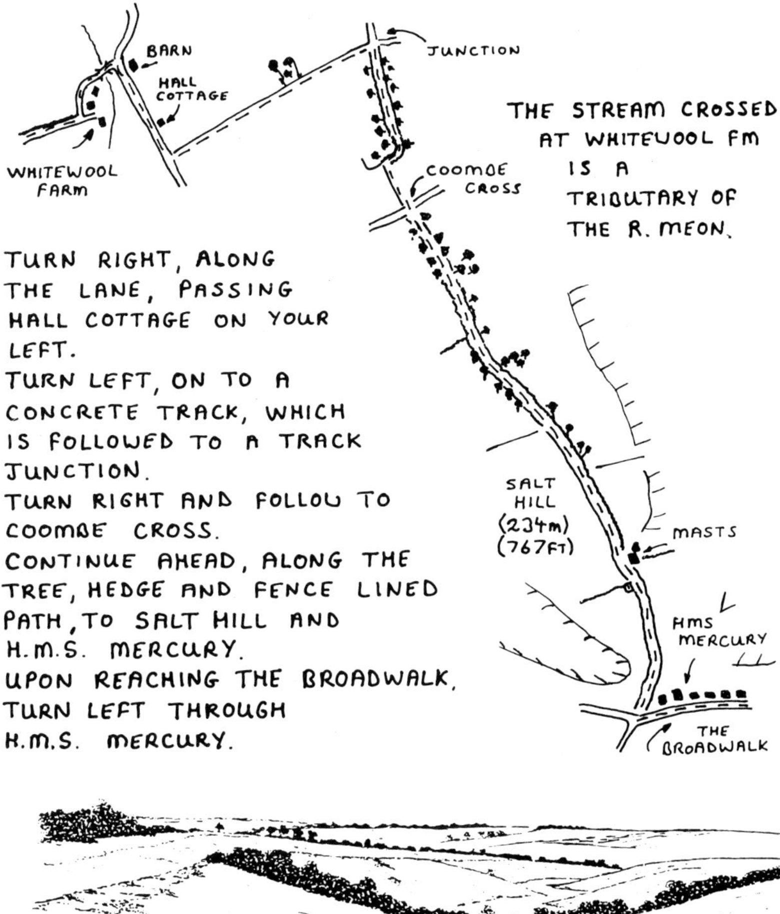

THE STREAM CROSSED AT WHITEWOOL FM IS A TRIBUTARY OF THE R. MEON.

TURN RIGHT, ALONG THE LANE, PASSING HALL COTTAGE ON YOUR LEFT.
TURN LEFT, ON TO A CONCRETE TRACK, WHICH IS FOLLOWED TO A TRACK JUNCTION.
TURN RIGHT AND FOLLOW TO COOMBE CROSS.
CONTINUE AHEAD, ALONG THE TREE, HEDGE AND FENCE LINED PATH, TO SALT HILL AND H.M.S. MERCURY.
UPON REACHING THE BROADWALK, TURN LEFT THROUGH H.M.S. MERCURY.

LOOKING S.W. FROM PATH, PRIOR TO JUNCTION WITH BROADWALK.

HYDEN, TEGDOWN AND BUTSER HILLS FROM HYDEN CROSS.

AN EASY PATH TO FOLLOW, WITH SPECTACULAR VIEWS TO THE NORTH.

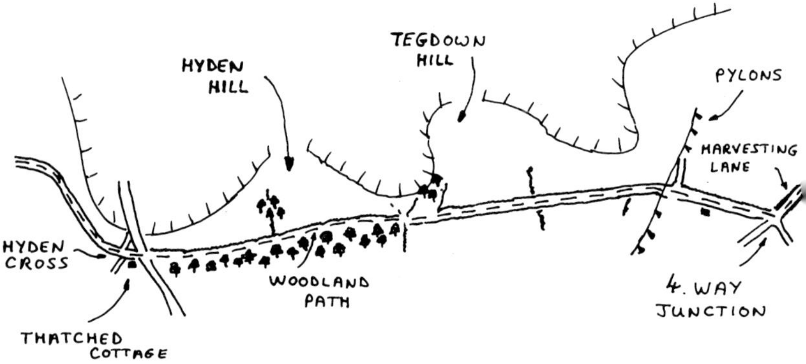

CONTINUE ALONG THE BROADWALK TO THE ROAD JUNCTION AT HYDEN CROSS.

CROSS THE ROAD, BESIDE THE THATCHED COTTAGE, AND FOLLOW THE WOODLAND TRACK OPPOSITE TO HYDEN AND TEGDOWN HILLS.

UPON REACHING A 4 WAY ROAD JUNCTION, TURN LEFT ALONG HARVESTING LANE.

QUEEN ELIZABETH COUNTRY PARK

LOOKING SOUTH OVER THE COUNTRY PARK, AND A3 FROM BUTSER HILL.

FOLLOW THE BLUE TOPPED POSTS TO THE A3 UNDERPASS AND VISITOR CENTRE.

APPROACHING BUTSER HILL FROM LIMEKILN LANE.
AT 270 METRES (886 FEET) BUTSER HILL IS THE HIGHEST POINT OF THE WALK.

HARVESTING LANE LEADS TO LIMEKILN LANE AND ON TO BUTSER HILL.

A LINE OF BLUE TOPPED POLES, GUIDE THE SOUTH DOWNS WAY AROUND TO THE RIGHT, AND DESCENDS TO HILHAMPTON BOTTOM, THE A3 UNDERPASS AND VISITOR CENTRE.

A NUMBER OF PATHS EXIST AROUND THE VISITOR CENTRE, ANY IN A SOUTHERLY DIRECTION WILL LEAD TO THE ROAD AND TRACK JUNCTION AT THE FOOT OF GRAVEL HILL.

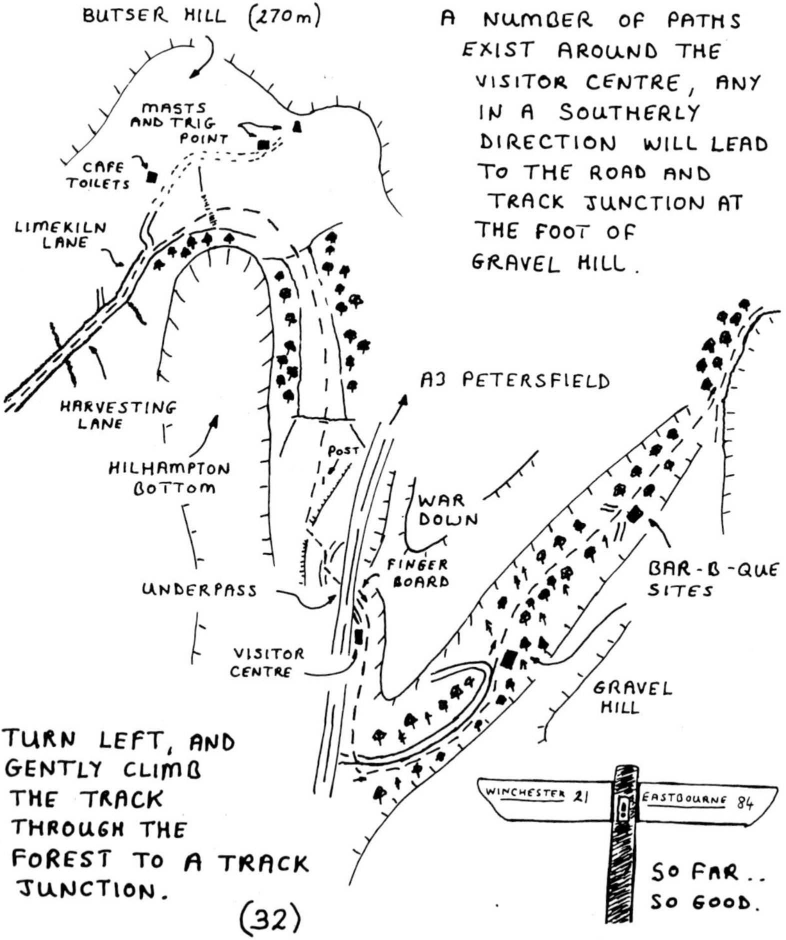

TURN LEFT, AND GENTLY CLIMB THE TRACK THROUGH THE FOREST TO A TRACK JUNCTION.

SO FAR.. SO GOOD.

THE QUEEN ELIZABETH COUNTRY PARK

THE VISITOR CENTRE.

OPENED OFFICIALLY BY THE QUEEN ON THE 2ND AUG 1976, THESE 1400 ACRES OF OUTSTANDING NATURAL BEAUTY ARE A HAVEN OF PEACE BESIDE THE RELENTLESS TRAFFIC OF THE A3. TRACKS, FOOTPATHS AND TRAILS LEAD IN ALL DIRECTIONS TO AN ASSORTMENT OF WOODLAND AND OPEN TOP VIEWS, INCLUDING THE SOLENT AND ISLE OF WIGHT TO THE SOUTH AND THE SUSSEX WEALD TO THE NORTH.

SPECIAL ACTIVITIES AND DEMONSTRATIONS ARE AVAILABLE, ALONG WITH THE VISITOR CENTRES DISPLAYS AND INFORMATION.

THE HAMPSHIRE COUNTY COUNCIL HAS BEEN VERY ACTIVE WITH THE INITIATION OF LONG DISTANCE PATHS, TWO OF WHICH START IN THE PARK.

<u>THE STAUNTON WAY</u> IS 12 MILES SOUTH TO LANGSTONE HARBOUR

<u>THE HANGERS WAY</u> IS 21 MILES NORTH TO ALTON.

QUEEN ELIZABETH COUNTRY PARK

BUTSER HILL AND HILHAMPTON BOTTOM

FOLLOW THE BLUE TOPPED POSTS FOR ACCURATE NAVIGATION FROM BUTSER HILL TO THE VISITOR CENTRE.

THE TRACK THROUGH GRAVELHILL BOTTOM IS PUNCTUATED BY MANY CYCLE AND HORSE TRAILS.

ONE OF TWO BAR-B-QUE SITES TO BE FOUND ALONG THE WAY.

CONTINUE ALONG THE TRACK TO THE CAR PARK AND ROAD JUNCTION BESIDE FAGGS FARM. TURN LEFT AND DESCEND KILN LANE TO BURITON.

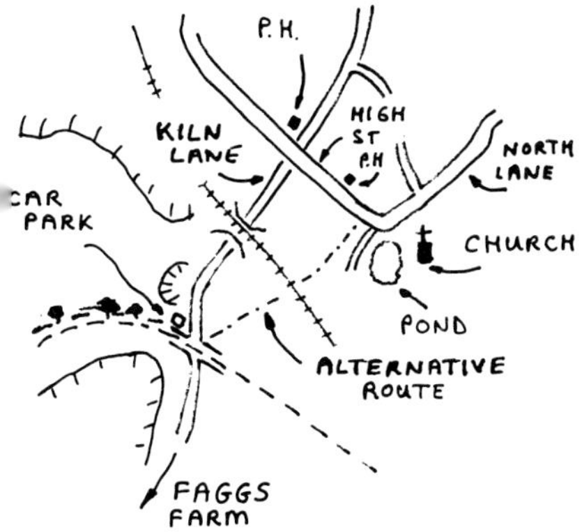

A PATH FROM THE JUNCTION, THROUGH THE WOODS, VIA THE RAILWAY AND CRICKET PITCH, IS A TRAFFIC FREE ALTERNATIVE.

BURITON CHURCH AND POND ...
ORIGINALLY THE START OF THE SOUTH DOWNS WAY.

BURITON

THE JUNCTION OF KILN LANE WITH.
BURITON HIGH ST.
BURITON HAS TWO PUBS, THE MASTER ROBERT AND THE FIVE BELLS.

THE SOUTH DOWNS WAY WAS THE FIRST LONG DISTANCE PATH AND, IN 1972 WHEN IT WAS OFFICIALLY OPENED BURITON WAS THE START, OR FINISH POINT.

THE CHURCH AND VILLAGE BECAME THE FIRST OR LAST PICTURE AND MEMOR FOR MANY WALKERS.

BURITON TO COCKING   11·5m   18km

B · BURITON
SH · SOUTH HARTING
BH · BEACON HILL
TH · TREYFORD HILL
C · COCKING

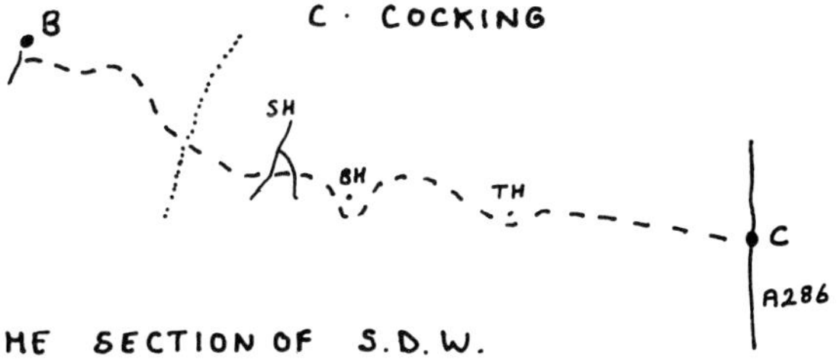

PRIOR TO THE SECTION OF S.D.W. FROM WINCHESTER BEING OFFICIALLY OPENED IN 1989, BURITON WAS THE EFFECTIVE START POINT.
THE CHURCH, POND AND VILLAGE HIGH ST ARE DELIGHTFUL.
A BRIEF CLIMB FROM BURITON ON TO THE DOWN IS REWARDED WITH AN EASY WALK, AND SNATCHED VIEWS ALONG THE ESCARPMENT TOWARD THE B2146.
FORTY ACRE LANE OFFERS THE FIRST VIEW OF S. HARTING, OF WHICH THE GREEN ROOFED CHURCH IS THE EYE CATCHER, AND FROM ALMOST THE SAME POINT THE RUINS ON TOWER HILL CAN BE SEEN.
FROM HARTING DOWN THE VIEWS ALTERNATE FROM NORTH TO SOUTH, AS BEACON HILL, PEN HILL, DIDLING HILL, LINCH DOWN AND COCKING DOWN ALL APPEAR ON A TWISTING BUT EASY PATH.
THE S.D.W. CROSSES THE A286 TO THE SOUTH OF COCKING, HOWEVER IF COCKING IS TONIGHTS B&B THEN A SAFER AND QUIETER ROUTE CAN BE TAKEN ACROSS THE FIELDS TO CRYPT FARM, PAST THE OLD RAILWAY LINE AND INTO THE HEART OF COCKING VILLAGE.

RE-JOIN THE S.D.W. AT THE JUNCTION BESIDE FAGGS FARM, AND TURN LEFT ALONG THE TARMAC LANE TOWARD APPLETONS COPSE.

CONTINUE ALONG THE TRACK, PAST COULTERS DEAN FARM, WHERE SIGNED LEFT AND RIGHT TURNS ARE MADE THROUGH COCKSHOT WOOD.

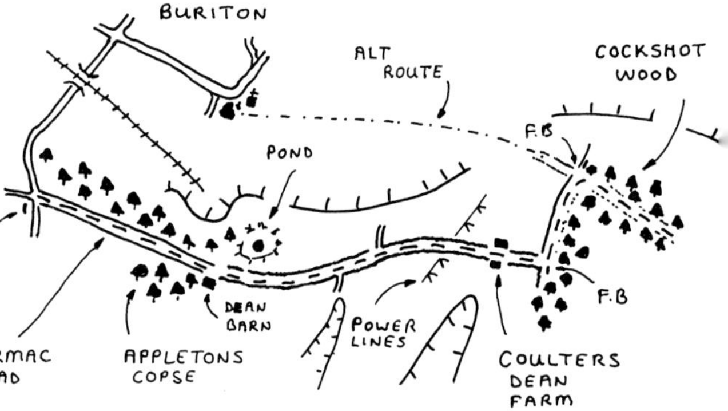

AN ALTERNATIVE ROUTE, MARKED ON SOME MAPS AS THE MILKY WAY, CAN BE USED FROM BURITON CHURCH TO THE COCKSHOT WOOD JUNCTION.

LOOKING WEST, FROM COCKSHOT WOOD TOWARD COULTERS DEAN FARM.

EMERGING FROM COCKSHOT WOOD, A TARMAC ROAD JUNCTION IS MET, BESIDE NORTH LODGE.
TURN LEFT AND FOLLOW A BEECH TREE LINED LANE TO SUN WOOD FARM.
TURN LEFT AND THEN RIGHT ON TO THE HEDGE LINED FORTY ACRE LANE, WHICH IS FOLLOWED TO THE B2146 ROAD JUNCTION.

THE COUNTY BOUNDARY BETWEEN HAMPSHIRE AND SUSSEX IS CROSSED 200 METRES ALONG FORTY ACRE LANE.

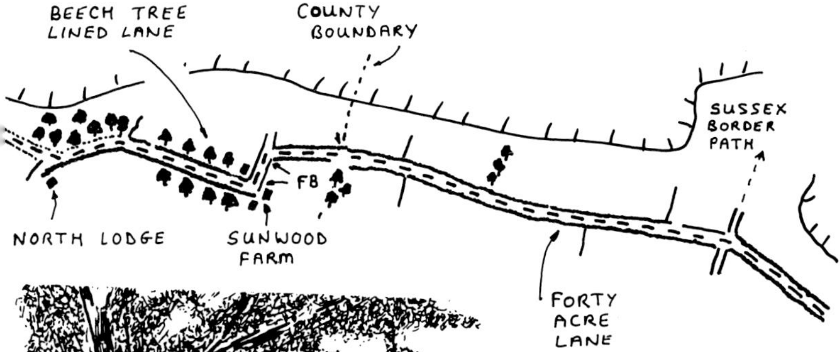

THE APPROACH TO SUNWOOD FARM, ALONG THE BEECH TREE LINED LANE.

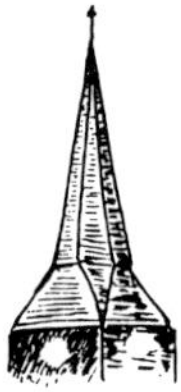

SOUTH HARTING CHURCH SPIRE

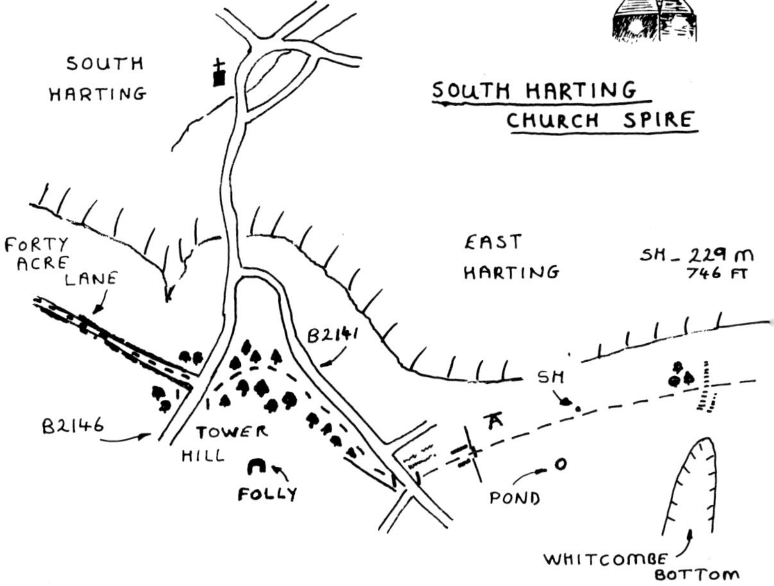

UPON REACHING THE B2146 ROAD JUNCTION, CROSS OVER AND FOLLOW THE WOODLAND PATH AS IT CLIMBS TOWER HILL TO TWO GATES AND THE B2141. CROSS THE ROAD AND CONTINUE ON THE WOODLAND PATH, SOON EMERGING ON TO OPEN DOWNLAND AND THE GENTLE ASCENT ON TO HARTING DOWN.

THE APTLY NAMED TOWER HILL HAS THE REMAINS OF A FOLLY ON ITS TOP, WHICH CAN BE SEEN FROM FORTY ACRE LANE AND AGAIN BESIDE THE B2141 CROSSING.
VIEWS OF S. HARTING, WITH ITS LIME GREEN CHURCH SPIRE, TO THE NORTH ARE COMPLEMENTED BY THE SOLENT AND ISLE OF WIGHT TO THE SOUTH WEST.

DESCEND FROM HARTING DOWN TO BRAMSHOTT BOTTOM AND THE FINGER POST.
TURN RIGHT AND FOLLOW THE TRACK AROUND THE SOUTH SIDE OF BEACON HILL.
TAKE CARE TO TURN SHARP LEFT AS THE PATH APPROACHES A SMALL COPSE AND TELEGRAPH HOUSE.
AT THE HEAD OF MILLPOND BOTTOM TURN RIGHT AND CLIMB PEN HILL.
DESCEND PEN HILL AND FOLLOW THE POSTS AROUND THE NORTHERN EDGE OF THE FIELD UNTIL A TREE LINED PATH IS TAKEN IN A SOUTH EASTERLY DIRECTION.

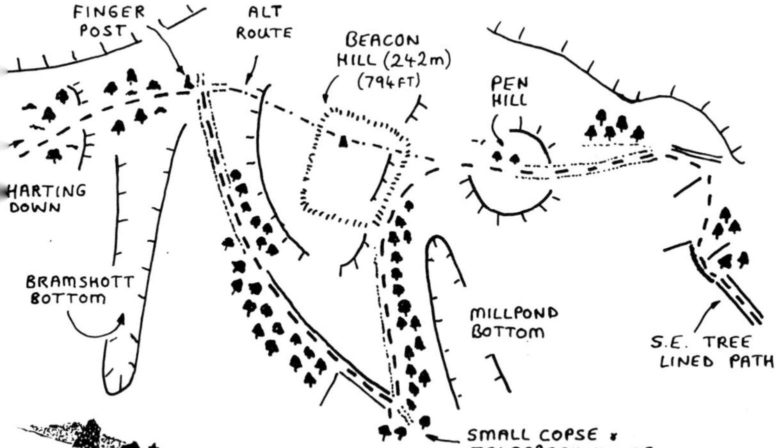

FINGER POST IN BRAMSHOTT BOTTOM READS:
BEACON HILL, HOOKSWAY S.D.W,
COMPTON, BURITON S.D.W.
EAST HARTING.

BEACON HILL

LOOKING WEST FROM PEN HILL TOWARD BEACON HILL

ALTHOUGH THE SOUTH DOWNS WAY BY-PASSES BEACON HILL, THE ALTERNATIVE ROUTE CAN BE SCRAMBLED TO THE TOP, AND AT 794 FT 242m THE VIEWS ARE EXTENSIVE.

BEACON HILL DISPLAYS THE REMNANTS OF THE OUTER EARTH RAMPARTS OF AN IRON AGE FORT.
THE EARTHWORKS, ALTHOUGH DIFFICULT TO SEE NOW, EXTEND FROM BEACON HILL, UP AND OVER PEN HILL.

UPON REACHING THE LANE SERVING BURITON FARM, TURN LEFT AND THEN RIGHT INTO A FURTHER HEDGE LINED TRACK.

THE TRACK IS FOLLOWED, PAST A CHALK PIT, AND THROUGH A WOOD TO A MEMORIAL STONE AND PATH JUNCTION.

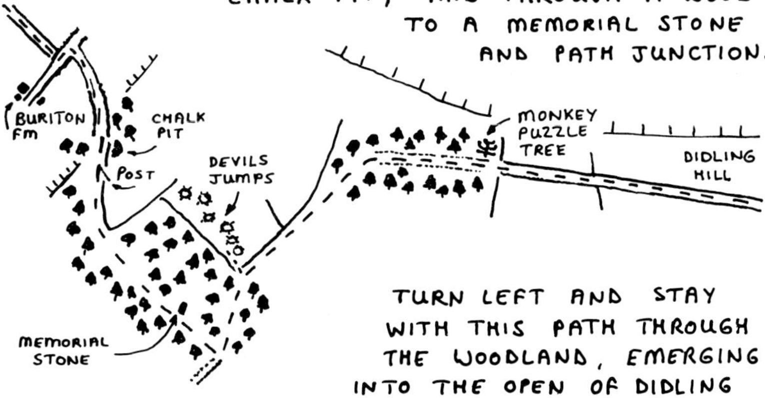

TURN LEFT AND STAY WITH THIS PATH THROUGH THE WOODLAND, EMERGING INTO THE OPEN OF DIDLING HILL BESIDE A MONKEY PUZZLE TREE.

NB. LOOK FOR THE WOODED PATH THAT LEADS TO THE DEVILS JUMPS 300m FROM PATH JUNCTION.

MEMORIAL STONE

RESEARCH WOULD SUGGEST THAT HAUPTMANN (CAPTAIN) JOSEPH OESTERMANN WAS SHOT DOWN ON 13 AUG 1940 BY THE TANGMERE HURRICANE SQUADRON WHILST ON A BOMBING RAID ON FARNBOROUGH IN A JUNKERS JU88A.

3 CREW SURVIVED.

MEMORIAL TO
HAUPTMAN JOSEPH OESTERMANN 1915-1940

THE DEVILS JUMPS

THE DEVILS JUMPS ARE VERY EASY TO MISS AS ONLY A FINGERBOARD MARKS THE WAY THROUGH THE TREES TO THE CLEARING.

THE NAME, ONCE AGAIN, OWES MORE TO FOLK LORE THAN TO ARCHAEOLOGY. HOWEVER THE SCENE OF FIVE LARGE BURIAL MOUNDS DATING BETWEEN 2000 AND 800 BC IS WORTHY OF SUCH BELIEFS.

AN INFORMATION BOARD OFFERS EXPLANATION OF THE WAYS OF THESE ANCIENT PEOPLES, AND A WALK AROUND THE MOUNDS INVOKES A FEELING OF RESPECT FOR THE WAY THEY TREATED AND RESPECTED THEIR DECEASED.

VIEWS OVER TO INK, BEACON AND BUTSER HILLS THAT HAVE BEEN OBSCURED BY THE PRECEDING WOODLAND CAN BE SEEN FROM THE END OF THE ENCLOSURE.

FROM A NAVIGATIONAL VIEW POINT THIS PAGE IS UNNECESSARY.... BUT IN THE INTEREST OF CONTINUITY

CONTINUE ON THE WELL DEFINED TRACK, BETWEEN THE FIELDS, OVER LINCH DOWN AND ON TO COCKING DOWN.

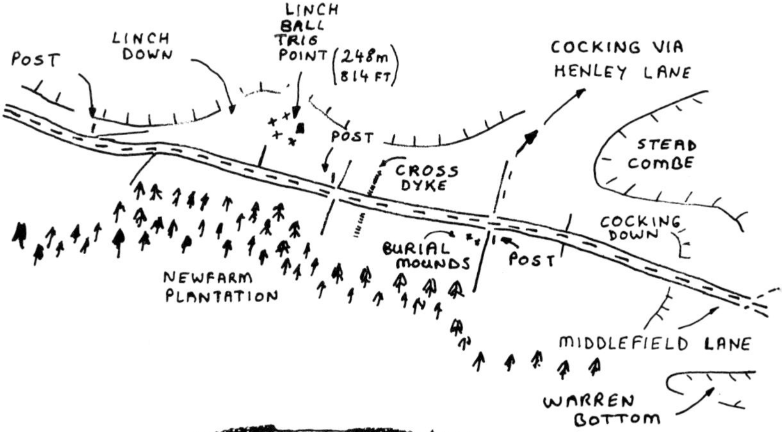

DESCENDING COCKING DOWN VIA MIDDLEFIELD LANE

THE GENTLE DESCENT OF COCKING DOWN LEADS TO TWO POSSIBLE ROUTES IN TO THE VILLAGE OF COCKING. BOTH ROUTES JOIN AT CRYPT FARM AND LEAD IN TO THE CENTRE OF COCKING.

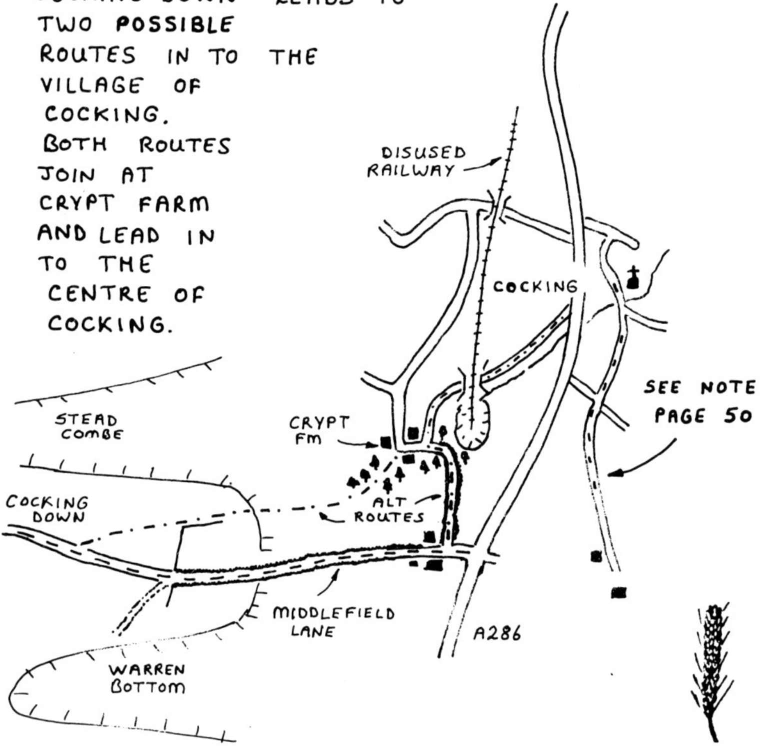

WHEAT

FOR THOSE CARRYING ON, THE S.D.W. CONTINUES ALONG MIDDLEFIELD LANE TO THE A286 ROAD JUNCTION.

COCKING

ALTHOUGH COCKING HAS THE BUSY A286 PASSING THROUGH IT, THE CHARM OF A SUSSEX VILLAGE HAS NOT BEEN LOST. A CHALK STREAM AND TEA SHOP ARE AMONGST THE FIRST TO GREET THE WALKER.

A RAILWAY BRIDGE, ON THE APPROACH TO COCKING, STANDS AS A REMINDER OF DAYS WHEN THE NETWORK SERVED MORE COMMUNITIES THAN TODAY.

LOOKING SOUTH ALONG COCKING HIGH ST.

COCKING

A PUB AND POST OFFICE STORE REPLENISH THE BODY AND THE RUCKSACK, WHILST A STROLL AROUND THE BACK LANES TO THE NORMAN CHURCH AND WAR MEMORIAL DELIGHT THE SENSES WITH THE TRANQUILLITY.

COCKING CHURCH

AWAY FROM THE BUSY MAIN ROAD THE CHURCH AND WAR MEMORIAL AWAIT.

INSIDE THE RESTORED NORMAN CHURCH CAN BE FOUND WALL PAINTINGS AND A TUB FONT, WHILST OUTSIDE ARE BEAUTIFULLY MAINTAINED GROUNDS.

COCKING TO AMBERLEY 12m 19Km

C · COCKING
A · AMBERLEY
H · HOUGHTON
R.A. RIVER ARUN
m/F/D · MANOR FARM DOWN
C/F · CHARLTON FOREST
G/D · GRAFFHAM DOWN
B/D · BURTON DOWN
B/H · BURY HILL

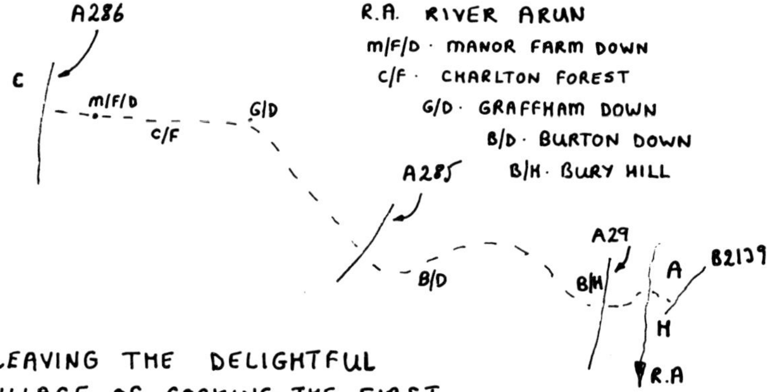

LEAVING THE DELIGHTFUL VILLAGE OF COCKING, THE FIRST CLIMB IS ON TO MANORFARM DOWN, AND SOME FINE RETROSPECTIVE VIEWS.
THE NEXT FEW MILES, AND THE ACCOMPANYING CHARLTON FOREST, MAKE FOR LIMITED VIEWS. HOWEVER THE SOUNDS AND COLOURS OF THE FOREST, WITH PERHAPS A GLIMPSE OF THE WILD LIFE, MAKE UP FOR IT.
THE CLIMB ON TO BURTON DOWN STARTS A SERIES OF FEATURES, INCLUDING CROSS DYKES, TUMULI, ROMAN ROADS AND NEOLITHIC CAMPS, WITH PANORAMIC VIEWS BOTH NORTH AND SOUTH.
THE S.D.W. CONTINUES OVER BIGNOR HILL AND BURY HILL TO THE A29 AND THE DESCENT TO THE RIVER ARUN VALLEY AND THE NEW RIVER CROSSING.
THE NEW ROUTE, WHILST BEING MUCH SAFER THAN THE OLD HOUGHTON RD, DOES MEAN THAT THE VILLAGE OF HOUGHTON AND THE AMBERLEY CHALK PITS AND TEA SHOP ARE BY-PASSED, BOTH WORTHY OF A VISIT.

COCKING TO AMBERLEY

THE S.D.W. CROSSES THE A286 TO THE SOUTH OF COCKING. HOWEVER SINCE COCKING IS AN OBVIOUS STOPPING POINT THE PATH NEEDS TO BE REJOINED BY FOLLOWING THE ROAD OR THE MUCH SAFER PATH FROM THE CHURCH TO THE JUNCTION OF HILLBARN FARM WITH HILLBARN LANE (S.D.W.)
SEE MAP ON PAGE 46.

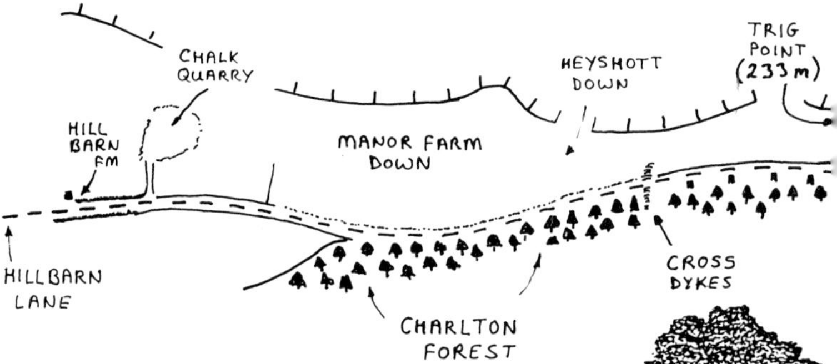

A ROUGH TRACK IS GENTLY CLIMBED ON TO MANOR FARM DOWN

OAK

THE S.D.W. IS ACCOMPANIED BY CHARLTON FOREST TO THE SOUTH (RIGHT) AND IS STRAIGHT FORWARD TO FOLLOW.
THE DISTANCE VIEWS OF THIS SECTION ARE SOMEWHAT LIMITED. THE ODD GAP IN THE TREES OR A WALK TO THE ESCARPMENT EDGE, VIA THE TRIG POINT, CAN BE REWARDING.

HEYSHOTT DOWN

THE WOODEN TOWERS TO THE LEFT (NORTH) OF THE PATH ARE THE REMAINS OF DEER SHOOTING TOWERS.

CLEARLY THE DEER IS A VICIOUS CREATURE, OF WHOM MOST WALKERS HAVE A TALE OF LUCKY ESCAPE WHEN ONE OF THESE CREATURES INDISCRIMINATELY DECIDES TO ATTACK. SARCASM ASIDE FOR A MOMENT, THE PROCESS OF ANIMAL MANAGEMENT IS A CONSTANT BATTLE BETWEEN THE BLOOD SPORT AND CONSERVATION LOBBY, AND THESE TOWERS ARE THE REMNANTS OF ONE SIDE OF THE ARGUMENT.

IF YOU ARE VERY QUIET, PARTICULARLY IN THE MORNING, YOU MAY CATCH GLIMPSE OF ONE OF THESE BEAUTIFUL CREATURES BEFORE IT SEES YOU AND RUNS OFF.

A NUMBER OF STONES CAN BE FOUND ALONG THIS SECTION OF THE ROUTE, BUT HOLD NO EXPLANATION. DISTANCE OR BOUNDARY STONES PERHAPS?

THIS SECTION IS LARGELY WOODED.
A BRIEF LEFT AND THEN RIGHT AT COOMBE BOTTOM PASSES THE CROSS DYKES AND MOUNDS, BEFORE THE WOODLAND PATH LEADS TO GRAFFHAM DOWN.

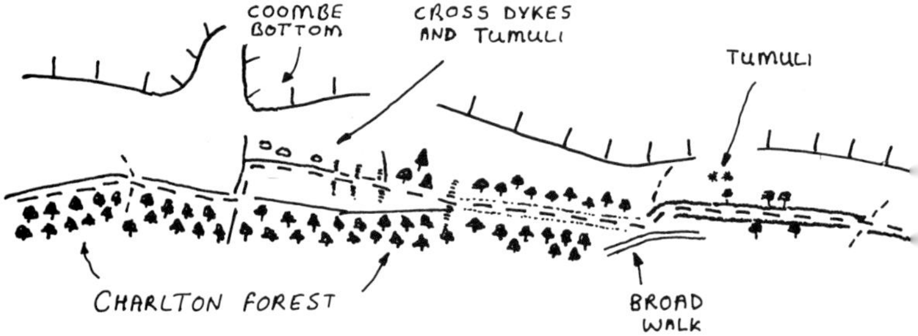

THE BURIAL MOUNDS AT COOMBE BOTTOM TO THE NORTH OF THE SOUTH DOWNS WAY.

THE S.D.W. IS VERY EASY TO FIND AND FOLLOW ALONG THIS SECTION.
AN OBVIOUS WAY MARKER TO LOOK OUT FOR IS THE BARKWORTH MEMORIAL, TO BE FOUND UPON EMERGING FROM CHARLTON FOREST.

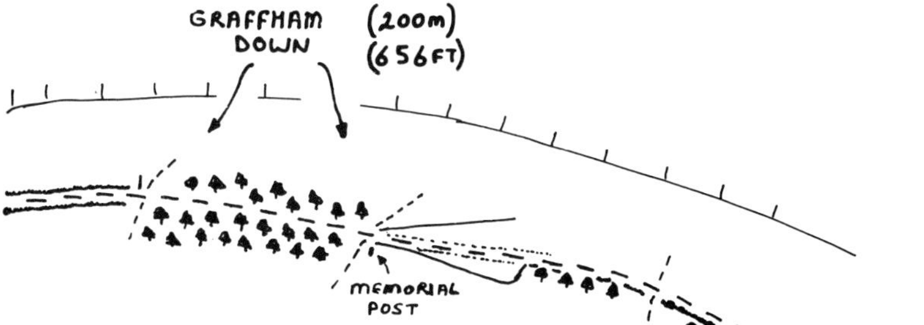

T WAS ON THIS SECTION THAT WE NCOUNTERED A BOTANIST, WHO TOOK THE TIME TO EXPLAIN WHY SPECIES ARE DYING OUT:
IT IS LAND OR MORE SPECIFICALLY FIELD BARRIERS THAT ARE CAUSING THE DECLINE.
WOODLAND HAS BEEN CLEARED, SO AREAS OF WOODLAND BECOME ISOLATED, AND THE WILD LIFE UITH IT.
WITH MANY SPECIES THAT CANNOT CROSS THE FIELDS THE COPSE BECOMES AN ISLAND AND THE CYCLE OF MOVEMENT, FOOD AND REPRODUCTION EVENTUALLY DECLINES.

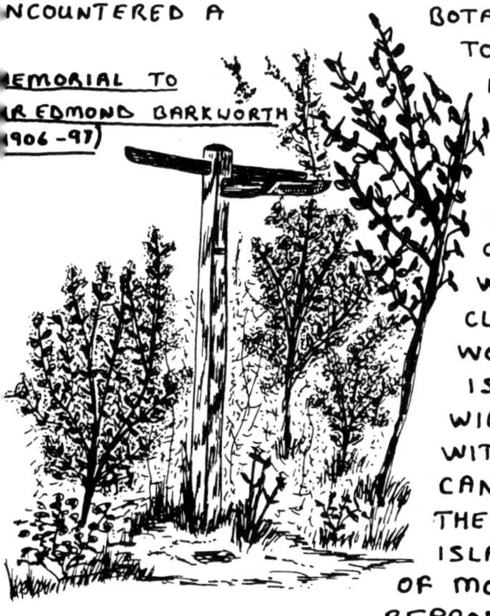

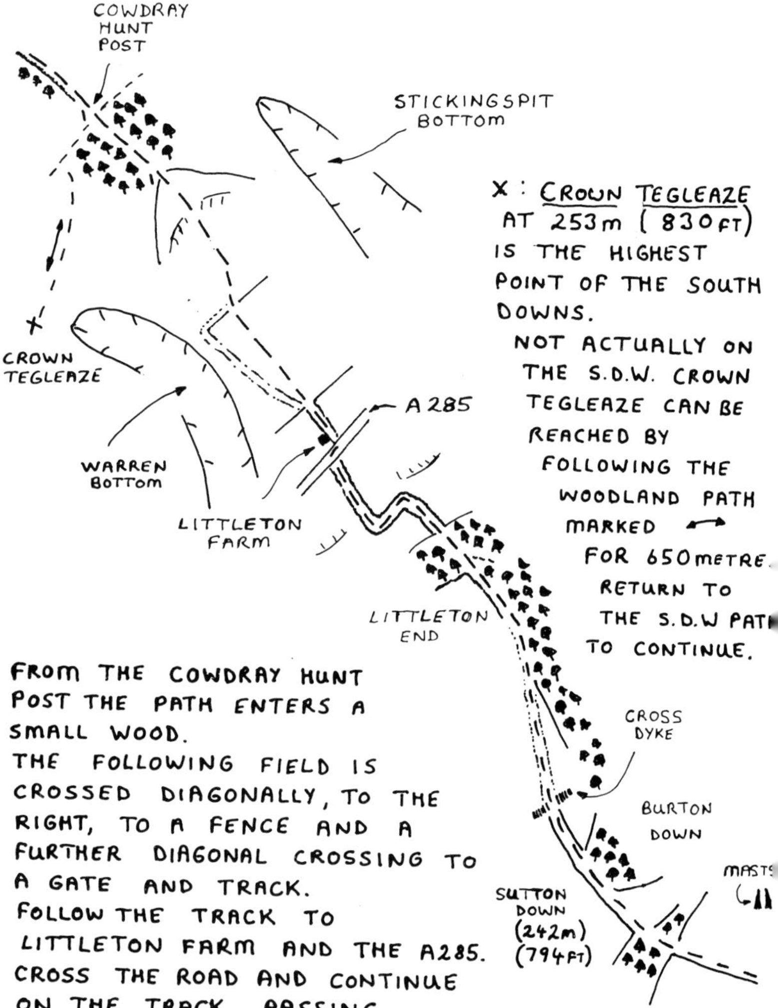

X : CROWN TEGLEAZE AT 253m (830FT) IS THE HIGHEST POINT OF THE SOUTH DOWNS.
NOT ACTUALLY ON THE S.D.W. CROWN TEGLEAZE CAN BE REACHED BY FOLLOWING THE WOODLAND PATH MARKED ⟷ FOR 650METRE. RETURN TO THE S.D.W PATH TO CONTINUE.

FROM THE COWDRAY HUNT POST THE PATH ENTERS A SMALL WOOD.
THE FOLLOWING FIELD IS CROSSED DIAGONALLY, TO THE RIGHT, TO A FENCE AND A FURTHER DIAGONAL CROSSING TO A GATE AND TRACK.
FOLLOW THE TRACK TO LITTLETON FARM AND THE A285.
CROSS THE ROAD AND CONTINUE ON THE TRACK, PASSING LITTLETON END, SUTTON DOWN, TO BURTON DOWN AND THE RADIO MASTS.

AFTER CROSSING THE FENCE LINED FIELD, THE S.D.W. GENTLY BEARS TO THE LEFT, FOLLOWING THE EMBANKMENT, ROMAN ROAD STANE STREET. TURN RIGHT TO THE LATIN WAYMARKER AND CAR PARK.

THE RADIO MASTS

CROSS THE CAR PARK AND BEAR RIGHT FOLLOWING THE S.D.W. ACROSS THE FIELDS.
A WAYMARKER, THE TOBY STONE, WILL BE FOUND AS THE S.D.W. ENTERS A FENCED SECTION.
UPON DESCENDING BIGNOR HILL A SHARP LEFT LEADS TO WEST BURTON HILL FARM. TURN RIGHT.

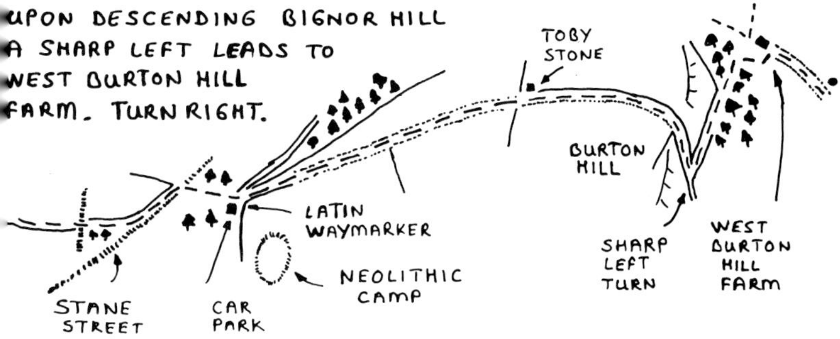

APPROACHING THE LATIN WAYMARKER, WHICH READS: BIGNOR, LONDINIUM, SUTTON, SLINDON AND NOVIOMAGUS.

THE ROMANS IN BRITIAN (43AD TO 410AD)

STANE STREET,

IS A ROMAN ROAD WHICH CONNECTED LONDON WITH CHICHESTER, FOR TRADING AND MILITARY PURPOSES.
THE EMBANKMENT IS EASILY SEEN AND FOLLOWED IN BOTH DIRECTIONS, WITH EARTHAM WOOD TO THE SOUTH WEST AND THE VILLAGE OF BIGNOR TO TO THE NORTH EAST.

BIGNOR

THE ROMAN VILLA AND SETTLEMENT REMAINED UNKNOWN UNTIL, IN THE EARLY (19), A WORKMAN UNEARTHED THE FIRST EVIDENCE.
FROM THEN THE SITE HAS BEEN ESTABLISHED AND EXCAVATED AS A LARGE FIND, WHICH WAS PREVIOUSLY OCCUPIED FOR SOME FOUR CENTURIES.
THE MOSAICS AND ROMAN ARTIFACTS ARE A MUST FOR THE CONNOISSEUR, AND A FASCINATING LOOK INTO LIFE ON THE DOWNS 2000 YEARS AGO.

<u>THE ROMAN ROAD</u>, STANE STREET, AND THE SOUTH DOWNS WAY.

CONTINUE ALONG THE FENCE LINED TRACK TO A PATH JUNCTION BESIDE A WOOD, ON THE RIGHT.

TAKE THE SIGNED (S.D.W.) PATH ACROSS THE FIELD TO THE A29. TURN RIGHT AND THEN LEFT, CROSSING THE ROAD AND BEGIN DESCENDING BURY HILL TOWARD THE ARUN VALLEY. THE TWISTING PATH LEADS TO HOUGHTON LANE.

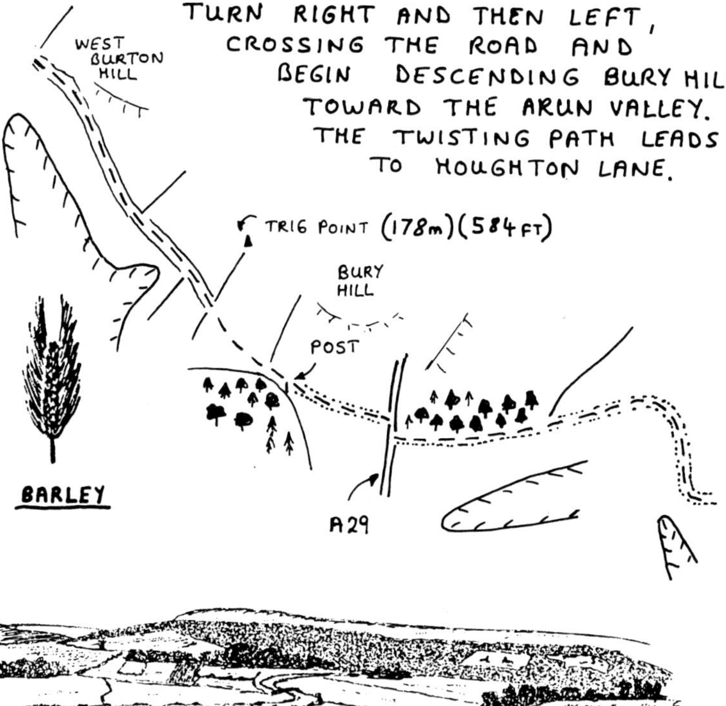

BARLEY

THE DESCENT OF BURY HILL TOWARD AMBERLEY IN THE ARUN VALLEY.

HOUGHTON LANE IS CROSSED AND A GRAVEL PATH FOLLOWED AROUND THE EDGE OF TWO SMALL FIELDS TO THE RIVER BANK AND THE BRIDGE.

CROSS THE BRIDGE, TURN RIGHT ALONG THE RIVER BANK.

TURN LEFT INTO A FENCED TRACK LEADING AWAY FROM THE RIVER, TOWARD THE TREATMENT WORKS AND OVER THE RAILWAY BRIDGE TO THE B2139.

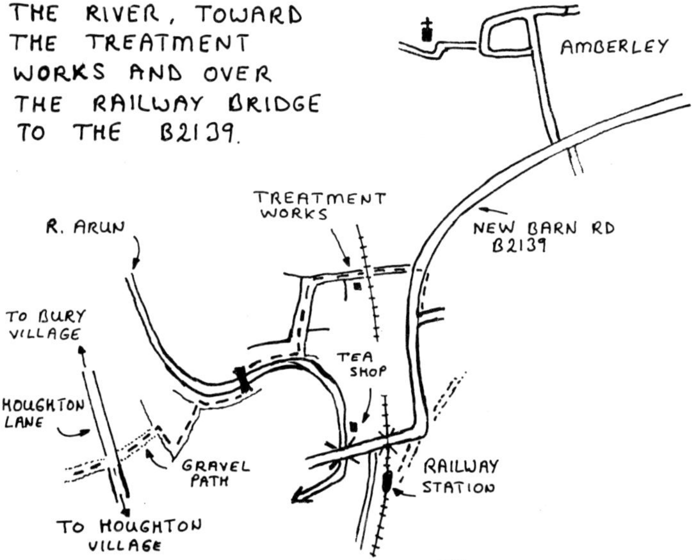

THE RIVER ARUN BRIDGE CROSSING

AMBERLEY TO WASHINGTON 6m 10Km

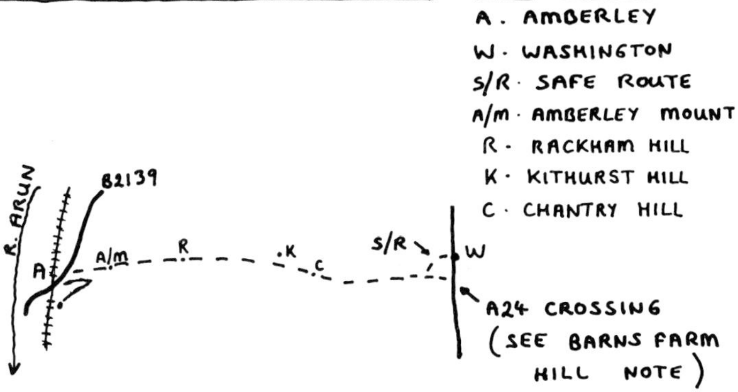

LEAVING THE BROAD ARUN VALLEY AND THE VILLAGES OF AMBERLEY AND HOUGHTON, A GENTLE CLIMB LEADS TO AMBERLEY MOUNT.
RACKHAM, KITHURST AND CHANTRY HILL ARE ALL PASSED ON A DAY OF ESCARPMENT WALKING.
THE EXTENSIVE VIEWS TO THE NORTH BEYOND RACKHAM HILL ARE A LITTLE OBSCURED, AND SO A ROUTE DEVIATION ON TO KITHURST AND CHANTRY HELP TO RE-BALANCE THE DAYS VIEWING QUOTA.
UPON REACHING BARNS FARM HILL, IT CAN ONLY BE STRESSED SO MUCH BUT, THE ALTERNATIVE SAFER ROUTE IS BY FAR THE BETTER.
ON THE APPROACH TO WASHINGTON, DO LOOK CAREFULLY FOR THE MARKER POSTS AS THE PATH AND A PRIVATE DRIVE RUN VERY CLOSE TOGETHER.

LEAVING AMBERLEY, TURN IN TO THE TARMAC LANE HIGH TITTEN AND FOLLOW, GENTLY CLIMBING TO THE ROAD AND PATH JUNCTION BESIDE THE HOUSE CALLED HIGHDOWN.

A ROUGH, FENCE LINED, STONE TRACK CONTINUES TO CLIMB TO AMBERLEY MOUNT. FOLLOW THIS PATH KEEPING THE FENCE TO YOUR LEFT HAND SIDE.

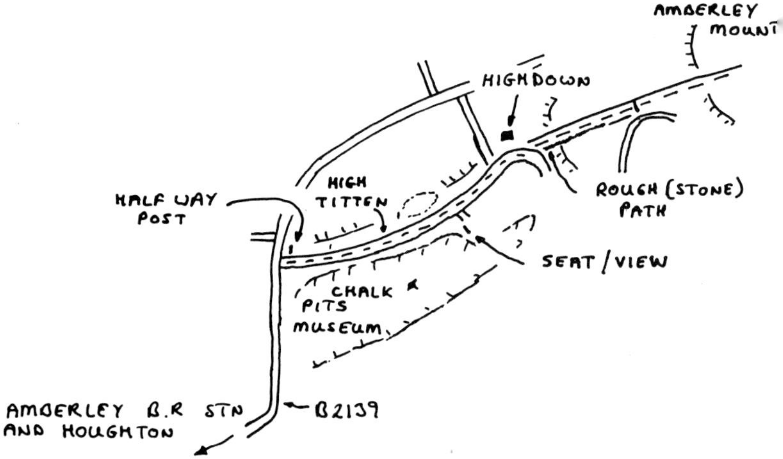

THE HALF WAY POST CAN BE FOUND AT THE JUNCTION OF HIGH TITTEN AND THE B2139

* THE CHALK PITS MUSEUM DOUBLED FOR SILICON VALLEY CALIFORNIA IN THE JAMES BOND FILM A VIEW TO A KILL

AMBERLEY

AMBERLEY CHALK PITS MUSEUM

ORIGINALLY AN OPEN CAST CHALK PIT UNTIL THE 1960s, THESE 36 ACRES HAVE BEEN TURNED INTO A FASCINATING INSIGHT TO LIFE, AND PARTICULARLY INDUSTRY, OF MANY YEARS AGO.

POTTERY, PRINTING, BOAT BUILDING AND BRICKMAKING ARE AMONGST THE MANY DISPLAYS, ALONG WITH A VERY PLEASANT NATURE TRAIL, AND OF COURSE A RIDE ON THE NARROW GAUGE RAILWAY IS A MUST.

REMARKS OF "WE HAD ONE OF THOSE" OR "I REMEMBER USING THAT" ARE COMMON PLACE AMONGST OLDER VISITORS, WHILST WIDE EYED FASCINATION OF A WORLD GONE BY IS BALANCED BY THE YOUNGER GENERATION.

THE PATH, MAINLY FENCED, IS EASILY FOLLOWED OVER RACKHAM HILL PAST THE EARTHWORKS AND TRIG POINT.

THE EARTHWORKS ON RACKHAM HILL

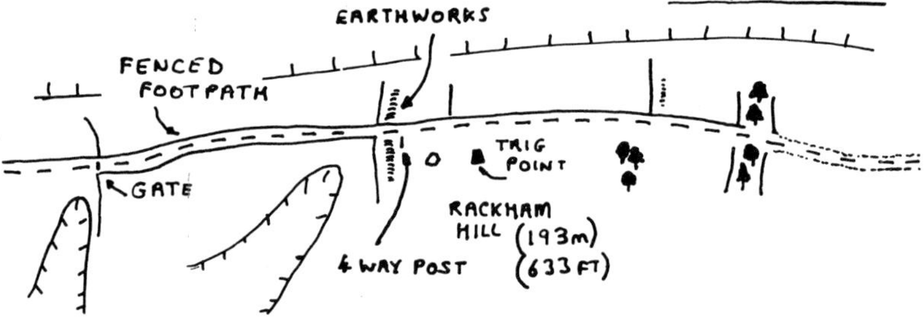

LOOKING WEST FROM AMBERLEY MOUNT TOWARD BIGNOR, WESTBURTON AND BURY HILL.

THE S.D.W. FOLLOWS A STRAIGHT FORWARD ROUTE ACROSS THE DOWN TO THE CHANTRY POST AND CAR PARK.

THE ALTERNATIVE ROUTE, VIA KITHURST HILL, AFFORDS GOOD VIEWS OVER THE DOWNS AND OF THE NORTHERN ESCARPMENT.

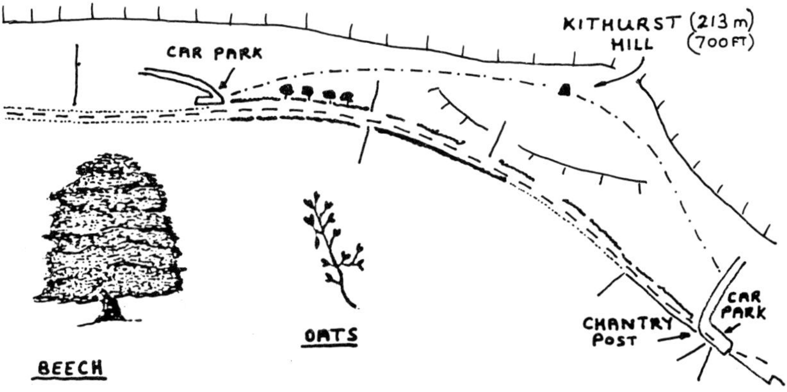

LOOKING EAST, ALONG THE SOUTH DOWNS WAY, TOWARD KITHURST HILL.

LEAVING THE CHANTRY POST CAR PARK, THE PATH CROSSES THE NEXT FIELD TO THE FENCE LINE, WHICH IS FOLLOWED WITH THE FENCE ON THE RIGHT.

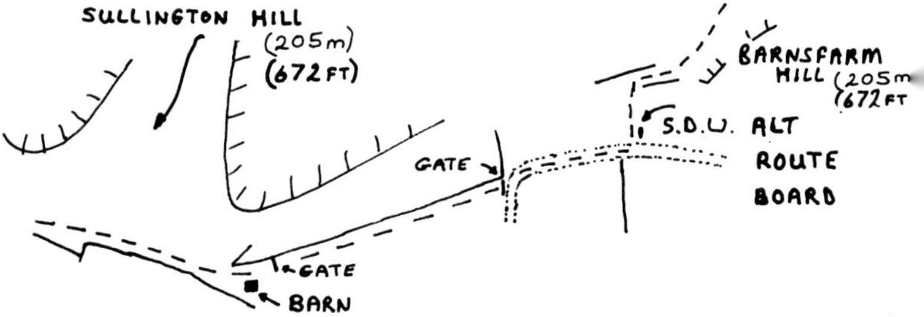

UPON REACHING A BARN, BEAR LEFT AND FOLLOW THE FENCE LINE, NOW ON THE LEFT.

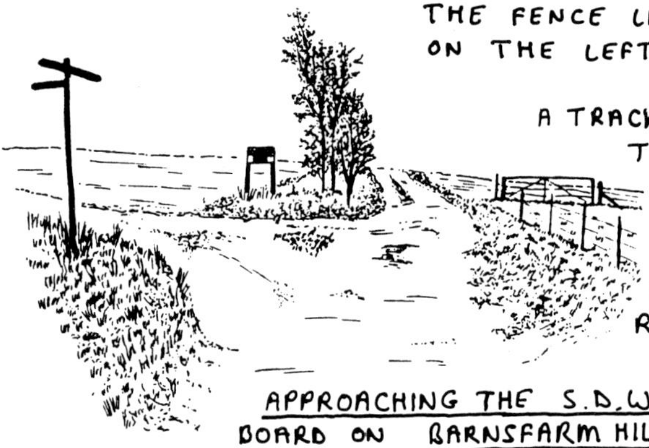

A TRACKWAY ACROSS THE NEXT FIELD BRINGS YOU TO THE S.D.W. ALT ROUTE BOARD

APPROACHING THE S.D.W. ALT ROUTE BOARD ON BARNSFARM HILL.

IT'S DECISION TIME

[S.D.W ALTERNATIVE ROUTE
SAFE ROAD CROSSING
← FOLLOW ←
EXTRA 2 MILES]

EITHER CARRY ON THE TRACK AND CROSS THE A24
(HEART IN MOUTH ETC)

OR

TURN LEFT AND FOLLOW THE SAFE ROUTE.

THE SAFE ROUTE.

TURN LEFT AT THE S.D.W. BOARD, AND CROSS THE FIELD TO THE FENCE LINE AND A RIGHT TURN.
THE PATH GENTLY DESCENDS THE DOWN, CROSSES A FIELD AND JOINS A TARMAC TRACK.
CAREFULLY FOLLOW THE PATH AND TARMAC ROAD AROUND THE COTTAGES, AS ONE OF THE ROADS IS PRIVATE.

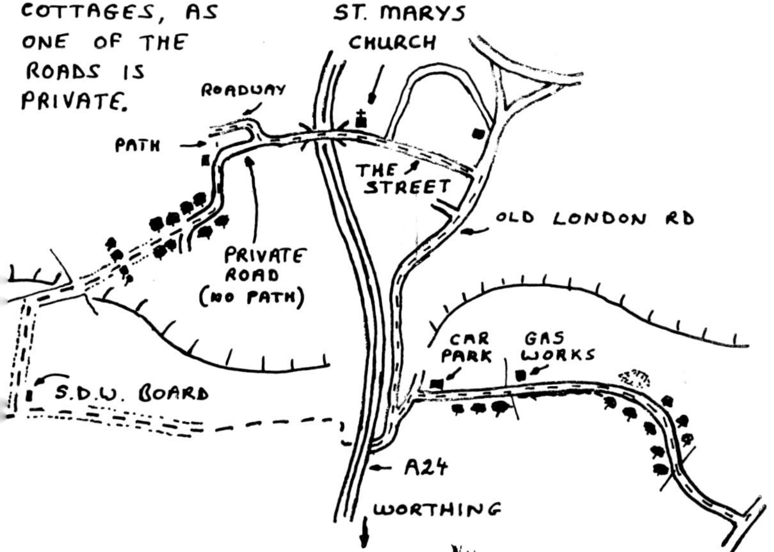

THE "SAFE ROUTE"
BRIDGE OVER THE A24 TOWARD ST MARYS CHURCH

WASHINGTON

THE CHURCH OF SAINT MARY'S IS THE FIRST VISUAL DELIGHT OF THE VILLAGE OF WASHINGTON.

THE FIRST CHURCH TO OCCUPY THIS SITE WAS BUILT IN THE 11TH CENTURY. SUBSEQUENT RE-BUILDS AND ALTERATIONS HAVE BEEN CARRIED OUT THROUGHOUT THE CENTURYS, INCLUDING ALMOST COMPLETE DEMOLITION IN THE 16TH AND 19TH CENTURYS.

IT SEEMS INCREDIBLE, IN THESE DAYS OF CONSERVATION AND PRESERVATION, THAT OUR PREDECESSORS WOULD GIVE THE ORDER TO DEMOLISH A CHURCH.

THE NEEDS AND REQUIREMENTS OF A COMMUNITY WER JUST AS EMOTIVE AS THEY ARE TODAY.

THE NAME WASHINGTON COMES FROM THE SAXON WORD WASA-INGA-TUN, MEANING THE SETTLEMENT OF THE SONS OF WASA.

A NUMBER OF SMALL SPRINGS RISE AT THE BASE OF THE DOWNS, INDICATING THE CHALK/GREENSAND/CLAY LAYERING.

THE A24, LONDON TO WORTHING ROAD, ONCE PASSED THROUGH THE VILLAGE WHICH IS NOW BY-PASSED.

WASHINGTON IS A GOOD S.D.W. STAGING POST WITH B&Bs, A PUB, SHOP, POSTING BOX ETC.

WASHINGTON TO PYECOMBE 14m 22Km

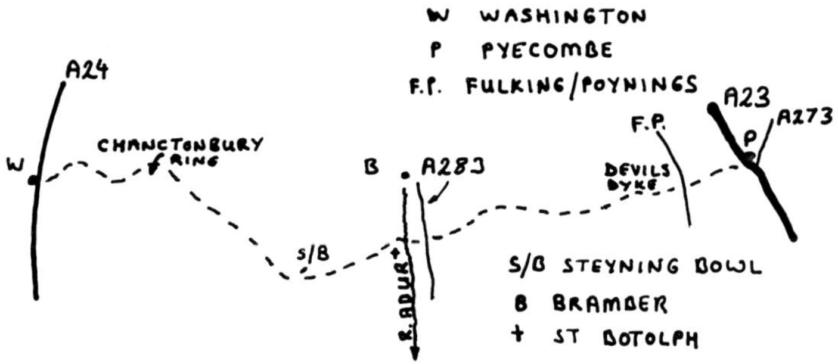

HIS SECTION OF DOWNS HAS BEEN BREACHED IN THREE LACES BY ROAD AND RIVER

HE FIRST CLIMB ON TO THE DOWNS, FROM WASHINGTON, REWARDED BY EXTENSIVE VIEWS ALONG THE SCARP ALK, AS WELL AS TUMULI AND CHANCTONBURY ING.

HE RE PLANTED TREES ARE NOW ESTABLISHING HEMSELVES AT THE RING AND AN EARLY STOP IS EWARDING.

HE DESCENT TO THE RIVER ADUR VALLEY IS VIA NNINGTON HILL WITH THE IMPRESSIVE STEYNING OWL TO THE NORTH AND THE PRETTY BOTOLPHS HURCH WAITING AT THE BOTTOM.

HE SECOND CLIMB OF THE DAY IS OF BEEDING HILL, ND ON TO TRULEIGH HILL WHERE THE UNDULATING ATH GENTLY BENDS AND TWISTS TO THE SECOND AGNIFICENT DRY VALLEY OF THE DAY .... DEVILS DYKE.

OR B&B IN POYNINGS AND FULKING THE PATHS AROUND HE DEVILS DYKE ARE THE CUT OFF POINTS.

OR THOSE CARRYING ON TO PYECOMBE IT IS STILL .... .. ONE MORE HILL.

VEST HILL IS A FAIRLY SHARP UP AND DOWN, BUT HE VIEWS OF THE DEVILS DYKE, NEWTIMBER HILL, ND THE ARRIVAL IN THE OLD WORLD VILLAGE OF YECOMBE MAKE IT WORTH THE EFFORT.

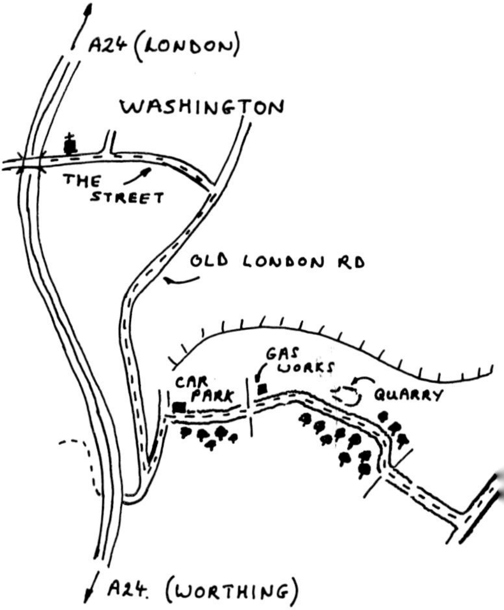

DIRECTIONS (SAFE CROSSING ROUTE) :

FOLLOW THE STREET TO THE OLD LONDON RD, TURN RIGHT AND CONTINUE TO THE A24 ROAD JUNCTION.

DIRECTIONS (A24 ROAD CROSSING):

CROSS, WITH EXTREME CAUTION AND PATIENCE, THE A24

TURN IN TO THE TARMAC QUARRY RD AND THEN RIGHT IN TO THE CAR PARK AND TRACK TO GENTLY CLIMB THE DOWN.
A SMALL QUARRY IS PASSED ON THE LEFT, AND A COPSE OF TREES BEFORE A T JUNCTION IS REACHED
TURN LEFT AND FOLLOW THE TRACK AND PATH TOWARD CHANCTONBURY RING.

THE DEW POND
TRIG POINT AND
CHANCTONBURY RING

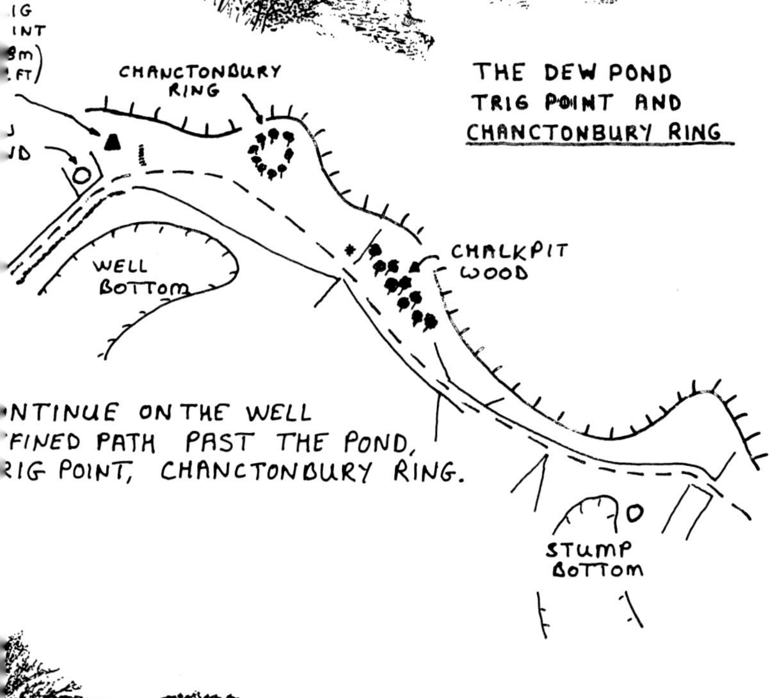

NTINUE ON THE WELL
FINED PATH PAST THE POND,
RIG POINT, CHANCTONBURY RING.

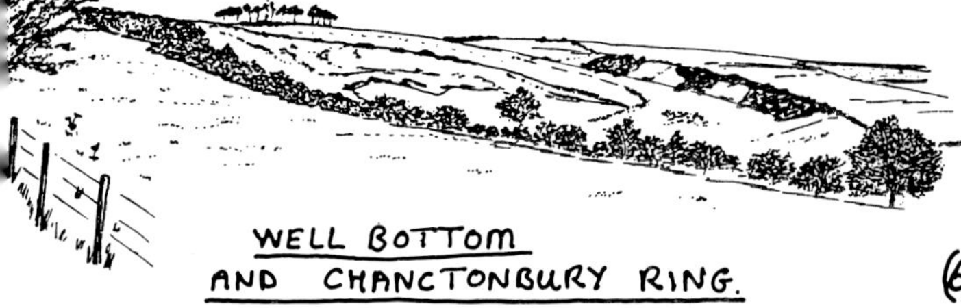

WELL BOTTOM
AND CHANCTONBURY RING.

ENVIRONMENTALLY SENSITIVE AREAS. (E.S.N.s)

AN E.S.N. IS AN AREA OF THE COUNTRYSIDE THAT THE MINISTRY OF AGRICULTURE, FISHERIES AND FOOD (MAF HAS DEEMED FIT FOR PRESERVATION IN ITS ORIGINAL STATE.

THE DOWNS OF POST WORLD WAR II DISPLAY A DIFFERENT LANDSCAPE FROM PRE.

THE REASON IS THAT LARGE AREAS OF THE ORIGINAL ROLLING DOWNLAND WERE PLOUGHED AND SOWED FO CROPS DURING THE WAR TO HELP FEED THE NATION. FROM A COUNTRY AT WAR POINT OF VIEW THIS WA VERY NECESSARY. HOWEVER WITH THE WAR OVER, AN THE TRADE ROUTES REOPENED, THE DOWNLAND WAS NOT RETURNED TO GRAZING WITH A RESULT TH THE STRUCTURE ALTERED.

THE ABSENCE OF SHEEP AND THEIR FEEDING PATTERNS, THE CLOSE CROPPING OF GRASS, PRODUCED A DECLINE IN MANY PLANTS, BIRDS AND WILDLIFE.

THE M.A.F.F. IS TRYING TO PERSUADE FARMERS AN LAND OWNERS TO RE INTRODUCE TRADITIONAL METHO OF LAND USE, WHICH RELY ON NATURES CYCLES OF GROWTH, USE AND REGENERATION.

THE SUCCESS OF THESE SCHEMES IS THERE TO B SEEN AS BIRDS AND PLANTS SLOWLY RE-COLONISE.

IT IS WORTH CONSIDERING THAT WHEN WE REFER TO T ORIGINAL DOWNLAND IN IT'S ROLLING GRASSY PASTURE SENSE, WE ARE ALREADY REFERRING TO A STATE THAT MAN ALTERED MANY YEARS BEFORE.

THE DOWNS WERE TREE COVERED FOREST FOR MANY YEARS PRIOR TO THE SHEEP FARMERS CLEARING THE TREES FOR THEIR PARTICULAR NEEDS.

WITH EACH AGE OF MAN THE COUNTRYSIDE HAS BEEN CHANGED TO SUIT OUR PURPOSE, AT THAT TIME, TO THE EXPENSE OF SOME AND THE SUCCESS OF OTHER WITHIN NATURE'S VOICELESS WORLD.

DEW PONDS

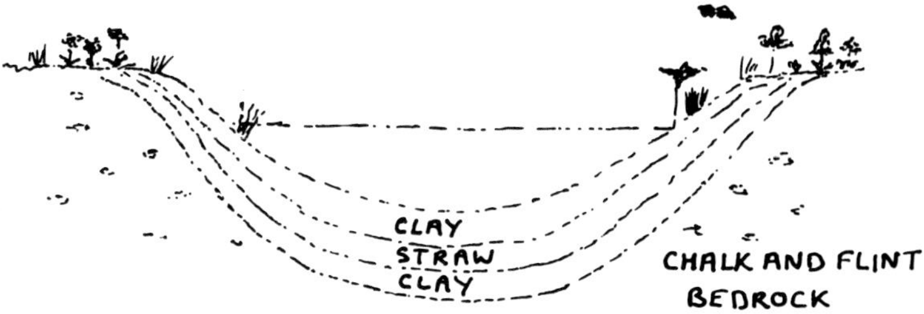

DEW PONDS HAVE BEEN CONSTRUCTED SINCE MEDIEVAL TIMES FOR THE WATERING OF GRAZING SHEEP ON THE DOWNS.
THE CLAY - STRAW - CLAY LAYERING WAS USED TO ENSURE A WATERTIGHT POND, AND WAS SUBSEQUENTLY USED BY THE CANAL BUILDERS OF THE 19TH CENTURY.
THE PROCESS IS CALLED PUDDLING.
SOME OF THE PONDS HAVE BEEN FENCED TO PRESERVE THEM, AND AS A RESULT HAVE BEEN COLONISED BY BIRDS, PLANTS AND ANIMALS.

CHANCTONBURY RING.

AT 238 M, 782 FT CHANCTONBURY RING COMMANDS A MARVELLOUS VIEW OF THE SURROUNDING COUNTRYSIDE, PARTICULARLY TO THE NORTH, AND PRIOR TO THE STORM OF 1987 BOASTED A SPLENDID RING OF TREES.
THE TREES WERE PLANTED BY CHARLES GORING IN 1760.
THE CLEARING AND RE-PLANTING AFTER 1987 HAS ALLOWED FOR CLOSER INSPECTION OF THE IRON - AGE CIRCULAR FORT ON WHICH THE ORIGINAL TREES HAD BEEN PLANTED.

FOLLOW THE PATH, PASSING A TRIG POINT ON THE RIGHT (WEST) AND A MEMORIAL STONE, UNTIL THE ROAD FROM STEYNING TO LANCING IS REACHED.

FOLLOW THE PATH, ON THE SIDE OF THE ROAD, TO A LEFT TURN ON THE SOUTH SIDE OF STEYNING BOWL.

CROSS THE FIELD AND EXIT VIA A GATE ON THE SOUTH SIDE OF THE BRAMBER BEECHES PLANTATION

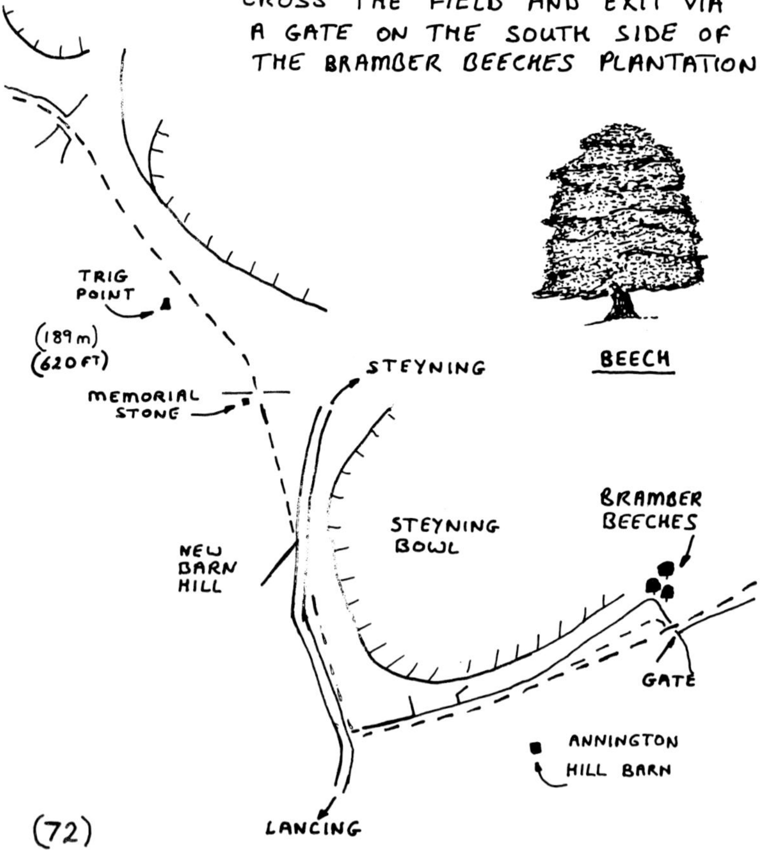

STEYNING BOWL

THE STEYNING BOWL IS A WONDERFUL EXAMPLE OF A DRY VALLEY, THAT CAN BE SEEN FROM MANY ASPECTS AS THE S.D.W IS FOLLOWED OVER NEW HILL AND ANNINGTON HILL.

THE BRAMBER BEECHES, AND MEMORIAL TO THE SUSSEX FEDERATION OF WOMEN WHO PLANTED THEM.

SOME GOOD VIEWS OF STEYNING, UPPER BEEDING, BRAMBER, THE ADUR VALLEY AND WINDING BOTTOM.

WITH THE DESCENT OF ANNINGTON HILL THE S.D.W. BECOMES FENCED ON BOTH SIDES RESULTING IN AN OBVIOUS GUIDING TO A TARMAC LANE.
TURN RIGHT AND FOLLOW THE LANE, PAST PEAR TREE COTTAGE AND ANNINGTON HOUSE, TO JUST BEFORE A SHARP RIGHT HAND BEND.
FORK LEFT FOLLOWING THE TRACK TO THE BRIDGE AND ON TO THE SHOREHAM RD A283
TURN LEFT AND FOLLOW THE SIDE OF THE ROAD FOR 250m WHERE THE CONTINUING SDW WILL BE SEEN ON THE OTHER SIDE OF THE ROAD.
CROSS CAREFULLY, YOU STILL HAVE MANY MILES OF DELIGHTS YET.

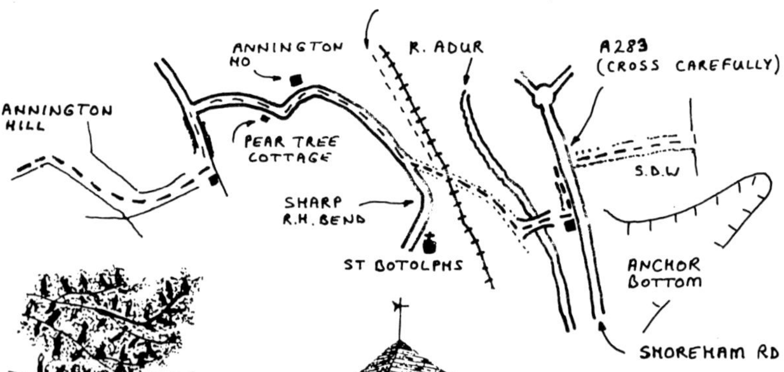

THE DOWNS LINK 1994 MARKER.
A PATH LINKING THE S.D.W TO THE NORTH DOWNS WAY.

ST BOTOLPH CHURCH.

SAINT BOTOLPH CHURCH

A BRIEF DETOUR IS REQUIRED HERE ALONG THE LANE TO: ST BOTOLPH CHURCH

ORIGINALLY CALLED ST PETER DE VETERE PONTE, MEANING "OF THE OLD BRIDGE", ST BOTOLPHS CHURCH IS ONE OF THE OLDEST IN SUSSEX DATING TO SAXON TIMES.

A WONDERFUL EXAMPLE OF A CHURCH EXPANDING, IN BUILDING TERMS, TO MEET THE NEEDS OF A GROWING POPULATION.

A DOOR DATED 1630, A JACOBEAN PULPIT, (16) BELLS AND (14) CHANCEL AND TOWER ARE ALL TESTAMENT TO THE PLACE IN HISTORY THAT THIS BUILDING HAS PLAYED.

PERHAPS ONE SAD EXAMPLE OF TIMES GONE BY IS THE "SLANT", "SQUINT" OR "LOW SIDE" WINDOWS WHICH ALLOWED UNWANTED PEOPLE, SUCH AS SINNERS, OR IN THIS CASE THE NEARBY RESIDENTS OF A LEPER HOSPITAL, TO SEE THE ALTAR WITHOUT ENTERING THE CHURCH.

COULD THIS HAVE BEEN A SIMPLE FORM OF DISEASE CONTROL, OR YET ANOTHER EXAMPLE OF MANS SOCIAL AND RELIGIOUS INTOLERANCE?

STEYNING, BAMBER AND UPPER BEEDING

THIS AREA HAS BEEN A RIVER CROSSING AND TRADING PORT FOR CENTURIES.

EVIDENCE SUGGESTS THAT A BRIDGE, FROM WHERE THE CHURCH GOT ITS ORIGINAL NAME, HAS BEEN IN EXISTENCE AS FAR BACK AS ROMAN TIMES.

COMMUNITIES GREW WITH THE AREAS PROSPERITY, AND DECLINED WITH ITS RECESSION, PRINCIPALLY DUE TO THE SILTING AND NARROWING OF THE RIVER, MAKING IT LESS NAVIGABLE.

THE SIX WAY JUNCTION

FROM THE SIX WAY JUNCTION FOLLOW THE PATH, BESIDE THE ROAD, TO THE YOUTH HOSTEL AND ON TO TRULEIGH HILL.

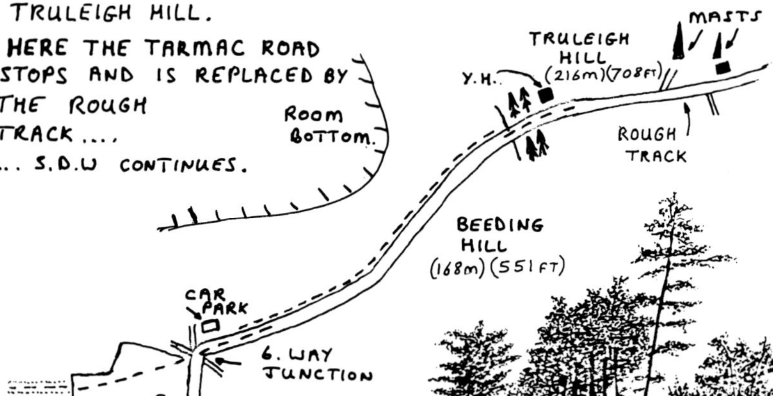

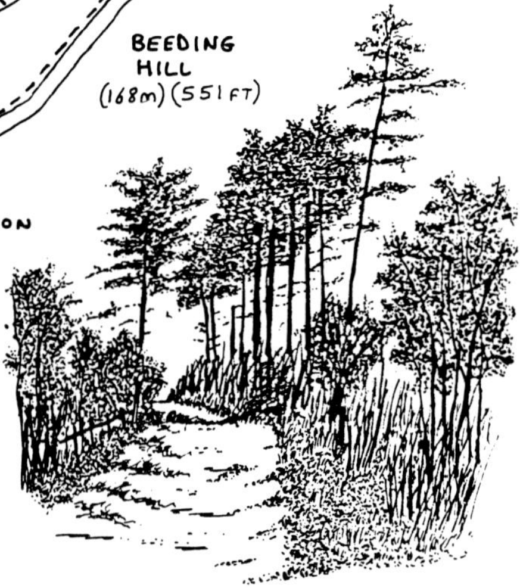

THE PINE TREE LINED S.D.W. BESIDE THE TOTTINGTON BARN YOUTH HOSTEL.

THE TRACK AND PATH ARE EASILY FOLLOWED OVER EDBURTON HILL, AND ON TO PERCHING HILL.

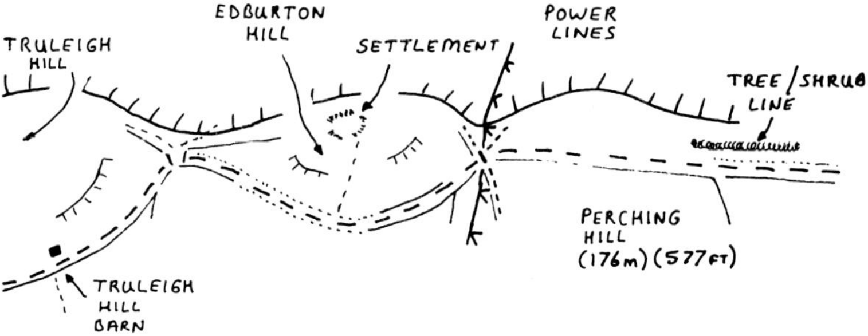

LOOKING WEST TO TRULEIGH HILL FROM EDBURTON HILL

APPROACHING THE DEVILS DYKE.

REMAINS OF THE IRON AGE FORT CAN BE FOUND ON TOP OF THE HILL, AND AT 217m (712 FEET) IS A GOOD VIEW POINT.

UPON REACHING THE TOP OF FULKING HILL, AND THE MAZE OF FOOTPATHS THEREON ... TAKE A MOMENT TO CONSIDER THE OPTIONS.
THE S.D.W CROSSES THE FIELD, LOOK FOR THE FINGER BOARD (F.B) IN THE MIDDLE, THEN OVER THE ROAD AND DOWN THE TREE LINED TRACK, BESIDE THE DEVILS DYKE TO THE ROAD BESIDE SADDLESCOMBE FARM.

AN EXPLORATION OF THE IRON AGE FORT, OF WHICH THE OUTLINE AND STRATEGIC POSITION IS CLEAR TO SEE.

FOOD AND DRINK AT THE DEVILS DYKE P.H.
SIT AND ADMIRE THE VIEWS

WALK DOWN, AND THROUGH THE DYKE.... A VARIETY OF PATHS CRISS CROSS THE WHOLE AREA.

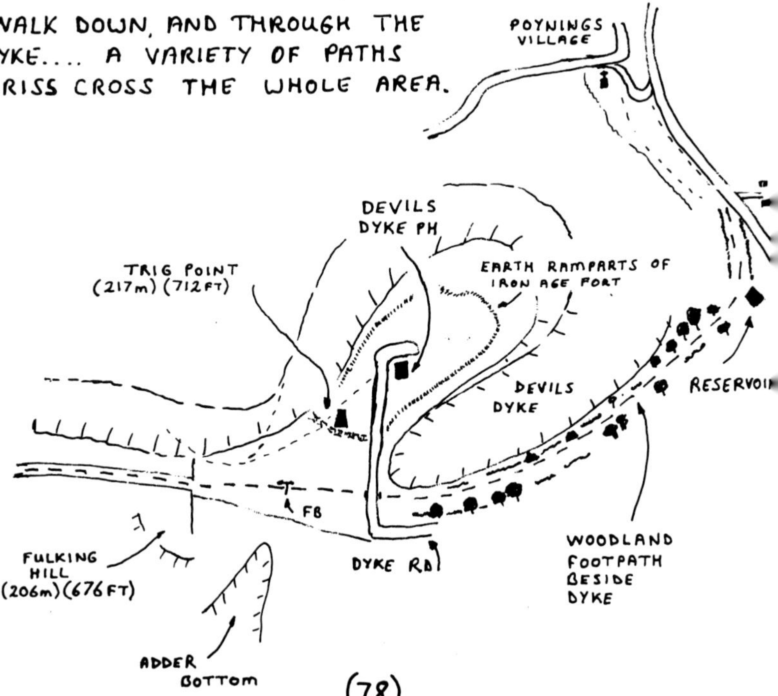

THE DEVILS DYKE

A VIEW FROM THE 'TOP' OF THE DYKE, LOOKING NORTH EAST. NEWTIMBER HILL CAN BE SEEN IN THE BACKGROUND.

POYNINGS, FULKING AND EDBURTON.

ALL THREE VILLAGES CAN BE REACHED BY A MYRIAD OF PATHS THAT DESCEND THE NORTH FACE OF THE DOWNS. ALTERNATIVELY A PATH ON THE WESTERN SIDE OF THE ROAD LEADS TO POYNINGS FROM THE DEVILS DYKE JUNCTION.

THE CHURCH AT POYNINGS, DATING TO THE FOURTEENTH CENTURY.

THE DEVILS DYKE

LOOKING SOUTH WEST
"UP" THE DEVILS DYKE FROM
THE POYNINGS TO BRIGHTON ROAD

THE DEVILS DYKE IS A MAGNIFICENT DRY VALLEY THAT IS ALLEGEDLY THE UNFINISHED WORK OF THE DEVIL IN HIS ATTEMPTS TO FLOOD THE WEALD CHURCHES FROM THE SEA.
CLEARLY FOLK LORE AND THE ICE AGE ARE AT ODDS ON THIS ONE, BUT THE VIEWS ARE SPECTACULAR FROM THE 217m (711 FT) ELEVATION, AND THE PUB A WELCOME BREAK.
REMAINS OF THE IRON AGE HILL FORT CAN BE FOUND AND THE WHOLE BOUNDARY WALKED, WITH ACCOMPANYING VIEWS OF THE WEALD AND DYKE.

CROSS THE ROAD AND FOLLOW THE SIGN BOARDS AROUND THE EDGE OF SADDLESCOMBE FARM.
NOTE: THE S.D.W. PATH NAVIGATES THE NORTH SIDE OF THE FARM NOT THROUGH IT.
PASS THE COTTAGES ON YOUR LEFT BEFORE PROCEEDING ON TO THE PATH THAT CLIMBS WEST HILL.
STAY ON THE WELL DEFINED, FENCE LINED, PATH OVER WEST HILL.

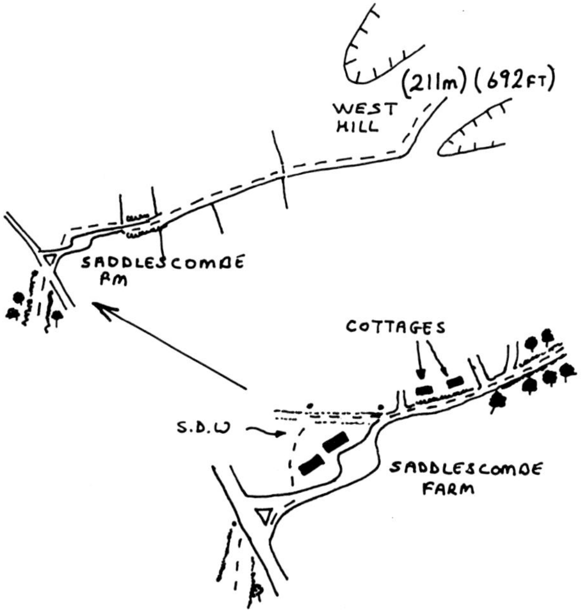

DESCEND WEST HILL TO THE PYECOMBE RIDING STABLES.
TURN LEFT TO THE A23 ROAD BRIDGE.
CROSS THE BRIDGE AND TURN RIGHT UP THE TARMAC LANE CHURCH HILL.
PROCEED THROUGH PYCOMBE TO THE ROAD A273, WHERE A LEFT TURN, ALONG THE ROAD, AND A RI LEADS THROUGH PYECOMBE GOLF COURSE.

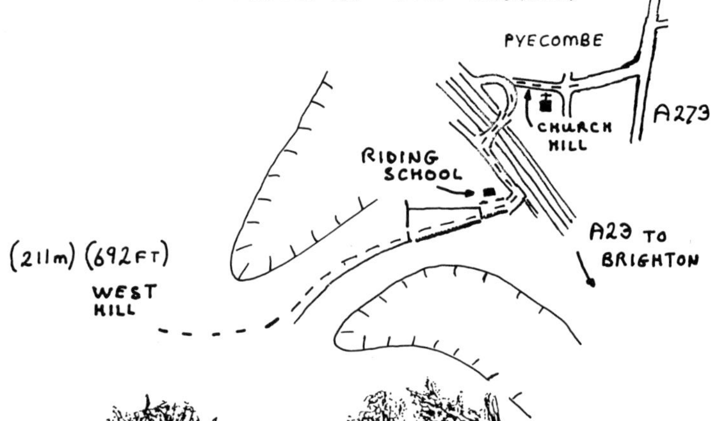

PYECOMBE CHURCH AND TAPSEL GATE FROM CHURCH HILL.

PYECOMBE

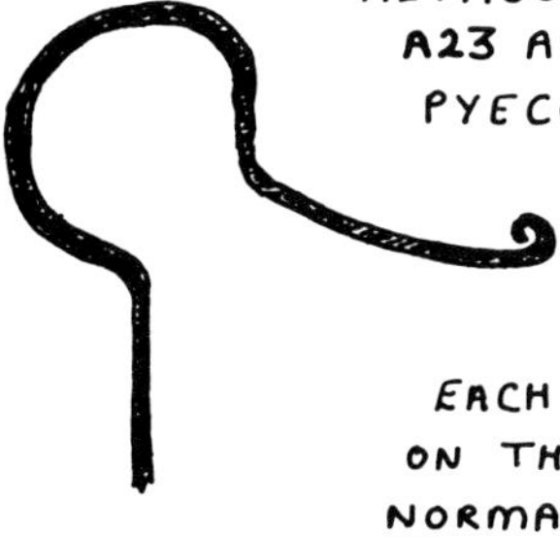

ALTHOUGH SANDWICHED BETWEEN THE A23 AND THE A273, THE VILLAGE OF PYECOMBE IS A DELIGHT.

THE S.D.W. FOLLOWS CHURCH LANE TO THE HEART OF THE VILLAGE AND THE 12 PARISH CHURCH.

EACH CENTURY HAS LEFT ITS MARK ON THE BUILDING, INCLUDING A NORMAN LEAD FONT, TUDOR WINDOWS, 15 BELL AND VICTORIAN RESTORATION.

A UNIQUE TAPSEL GATE LEADS IN TO THE CHURCH GROUNDS, AND EQUALLY UNIQUE IS THE SHEPHERDS HOOK THAT CAN BE SEEN ON THAT GATE POST.

THE HOOKS, THAT WERE THEN ATTACHED TO A SHEPHERD'S STAFF, WERE MADE IN THE VILLAGE BY A LOCAL BLACK-SMITH IN THE FORGE OPPOSITE THE CHURCH.

PYECOMBE TO SOUTHEASE 15m 24Km

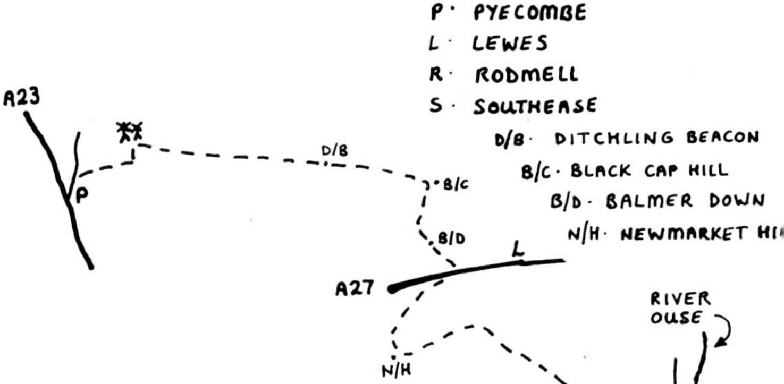

THIS SECTION IS THE LONGEST OF THE S.D.W. SO CAREFUL PLANNING OF TIME AND ACCOMMODATION IS RECOMMENDED, PARTICULARLY IF LEWES IS TO BE USED AS AN OVERNIGHT STOP.

THE WAY LEAVES PYECOMBE VIA THE GOLF COURSE, AND PROCEEDS TO THE WONDERFUL LAND MARK OF JACK AND JILL WINDMILLS, BEFORE A RIDGE WALK OVER DITCHLING BEACON AND PLUMPTON PLAIN.

JUST TO THE WEST OF BLACK CAP HILL THE S.D.W. TURNS SOUTH TO CROSS BALMER DOWN, ON WHICH AN ANCIENT FIELD SYSTEM CAN BE SEEN.

ROUTE CHANGE 1997

LOOK FOR THE NEW FENCED S.D.W. ROUTE THAT SAFELY CROSSES THE A27 AT HOUSEDEAN FARM, AND FOLLOWS THE RAILWAY EMBANKMENT AND THE EDGE OF LOOSE BOTTOM TO RE-JOIN THE ORIGINAL ROUTE TOWARD NEWMARKET HILL.

THE SECOND RIDGE WALK OF THE DAY IS EASY TO FOLLOW, AND WITH THE PATH SO CLOSE TO THE EDGE A REAL SENSE OF HEIGHT IS FELT.

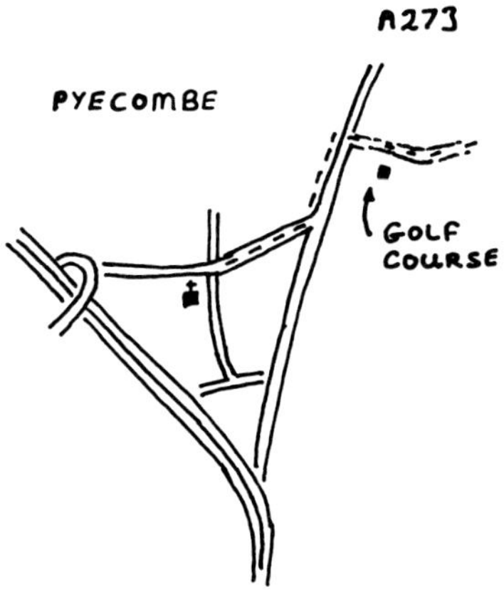

LEAVE PYECOMBE BY THE SIGNED PATH ALONGSIDE THE A273.
CROSS THE ROAD AND FOLLOW THE S.D.W. MARKERS THROUGH THE ENTRANCE TO PYECOMBE GOLF COURSE AND ON TO THE DOWN.

AS THE TRACK IS CLIMBED, THROUGH THE GOLF COURSE, TOWARD NEW BARN FARM, DO TURN AROUND AND LOOK TO THE WEST.
THE VIEW OF PYECOMBE WITH NEWTIMBER HILL (202m) AND WOLSTONBURY HILL (206m) IS A GOOD START TO A DAY OF ESCARPMENT WALKING WITH SPECTACULAR VIEWS.

THE S.D.W. AND TUMULI LOOKING EAST TOWARD DITCHLING BEACON

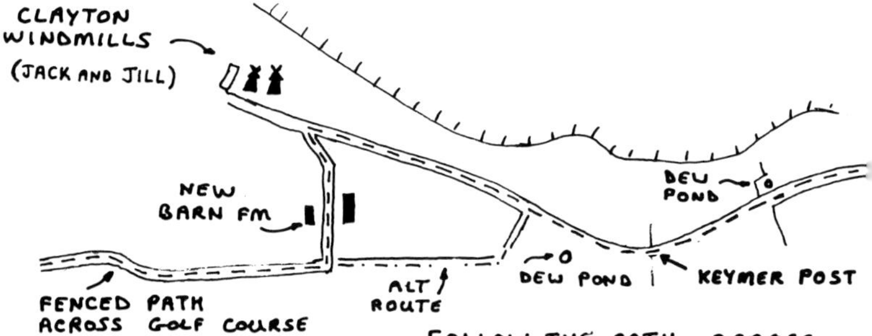

FOLLOW THE PATH ACROSS THE GOLF COURSE, CLIMBING THE DOWN.

TURN LEFT THROUGH NEW BARN FARM TO CLAYTON WINDMILLS, WHERE A RIGHT TURN IS TAKEN.

THE PATH NOW FOLLOWS THE ESCARPMENT EASTWARD.

JILL WINDMILL .... IS OPEN TO THE PUBLIC PERIODICALLY
JACK WINDMILL IS A PRIVATE HOUSE.
JILL WAS MOVED TO ITS PRESENT LOCATION AFTER ITS ORIGINAL SITE, AT PATCHAM, WAS FOUND UNSUITABLE.

THE KEYMER POST (235 m) (770 FT)

LOOKING WEST FROM THE POST ARE VIEWS OF NEWTIMBER HILL, WOLSTONBURY HILL AND WITH GOOD VISIBILITY CHANCTONBURY RING.

LOOKING EAST FROM THE RESTORED POST, WITH ACORN ON TOP, ARE VIEWS OF DITCHLING BEACON.

HE KEYMER POST MARKS THE BORDER OF WEST SUSSEX ITH EAST, AND INCIDENTALLY COMPLETES 75 MILES F THE SOUTH DOWNS WAY.

LOOKING SOUTH EAST FROM THE DEW POND TOWARD HEATHY BROW.

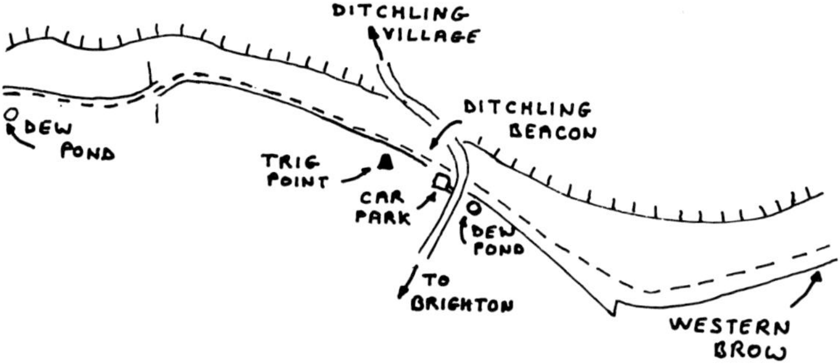

THE PATH, OFTEN WIDE AND WELL WORN IN SUMMER IS EASY TO FOLLOW OVER DITCHLING BEACON. CROSS THE ROAD, PASS THE DEW POND, AND CONTINUE IN AN EASTERLY DIRECTION ALONG WESTERN BROW.

<u>THE S.D.W.</u> AT <u>DITCHLING BEACON.</u>
LOOKING EAST TOWARD WESTERN BROW.

DITCHLING BEACON (248m) (813FT)

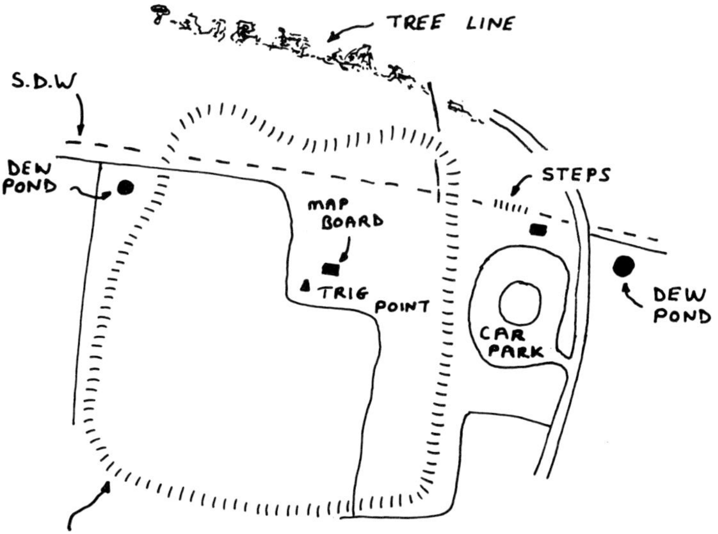

REMAINING EARTHWORKS AND BOUNDARY OF IRON AGE HILL FORT.

AT 248m THE HEIGHT OF DITCHLING BEACON GIVES COMMANDING VIEWS OF THE SURROUNDING AREA, AND WAS A LIKELY INFLUENCE UPON IRON AGE MAN TO BUILD THE HILL FORT HERE.

ALONG THIS SECTION IN PROFUSION ARE BURIAL MOUNDS, ENCLOSURES AND FIELD SYSTEMS, ALL ILLUSTRATING THE STRENGTH OF COMMUNITIES 2000+ YEARS AGO.

THE S.D.W. JUNCTION BESIDE BLACKCAP HILL

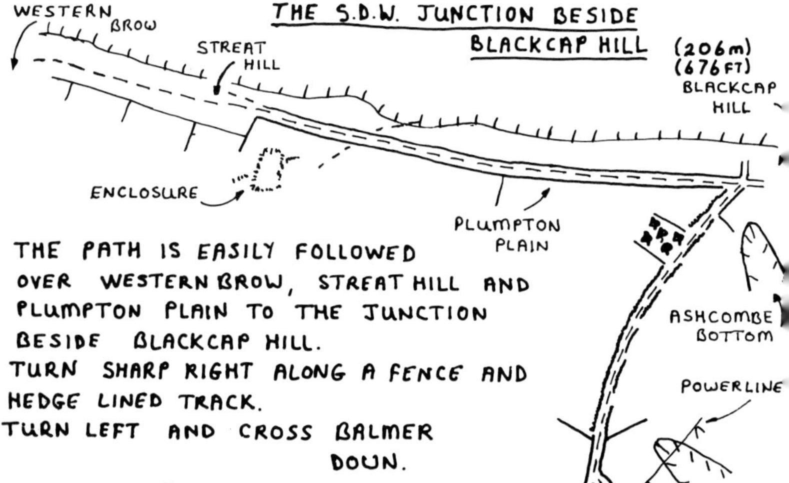

THE PATH IS EASILY FOLLOWED OVER WESTERN BROW, STREAT HILL AND PLUMPTON PLAIN TO THE JUNCTION BESIDE BLACKCAP HILL.
TURN SHARP RIGHT ALONG A FENCE AND HEDGE LINED TRACK.
TURN LEFT AND CROSS BALMER DOWN.

THE TRIG POINT ON BLACKCAP HILL FROM S.D.W. JUNCTION

WHILST DESCENDING BALMER DOWN THE S.D.W ROUTE TURNS RIGHT ALONG A FENCE AND HEDGE LINED PATH.

HOUSEDEAN FARM JUNCTION

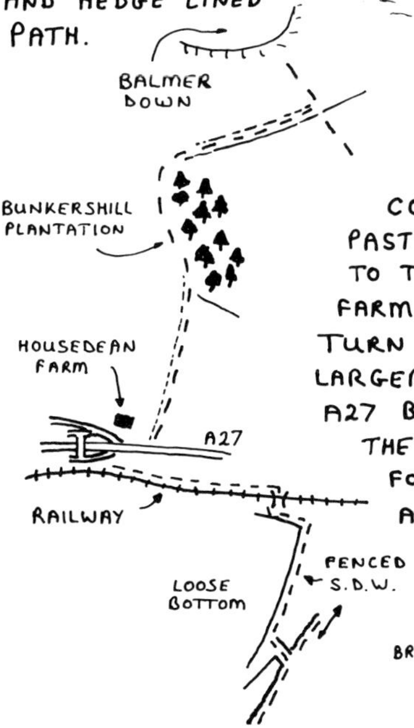

CONTINUE ALONG THE PATH, PAST BUNKERSHILL PLANTATION TO THE JUNCTION OF HOUSEDEAN FARM AND THE A27.

TURN RIGHT AND USING THE LARGER SCALE DRAWING, CROSS THE A27 BY THE BRIDGE.

THE FENCED S.D.W. IS EASY TO FOLLOW ALONG THE RAILWAY AND AROUND LOOSE BOTTOM.

THIS PARTICULAR SECTION OF THE S.D.W. WAS INTRODUCED IN 1997. THE ORIGINAL ROUTE CROSSED THE A27 1km TO THE EAST BESIDE THE NEWMARKET P.H. AND PETROL STATION. WALKERS REQUIRING SUPPLIES NEED TO BACKTRACK ALONG THE PATH MARKED ⟷.

APPROACHING COLD COOMBES AND THE NEWMARKET PLANTATION.

FOLLOW THE TRACK TO NEWMARKET PLANTATION. TURN LEFT AND FOLLOW THE ESCARPMENT AROUND TO THE LEFT TO KINGSTON HILL. UPON REACHING TWO PONDS, BEAR RIGHT ACROSS THE FIELD TO THE KINGSTON HILL DEW POND PROJECT.

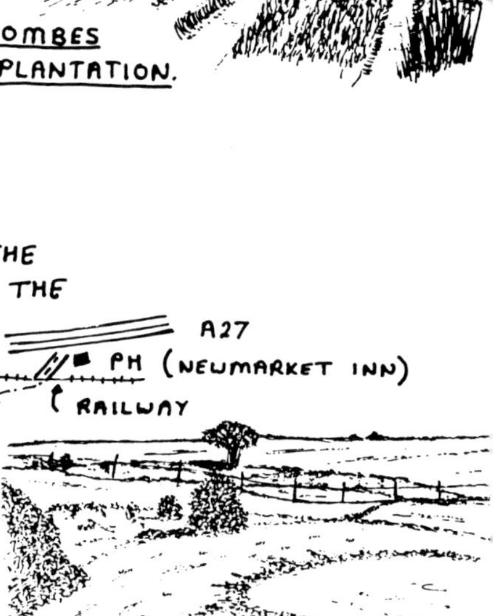

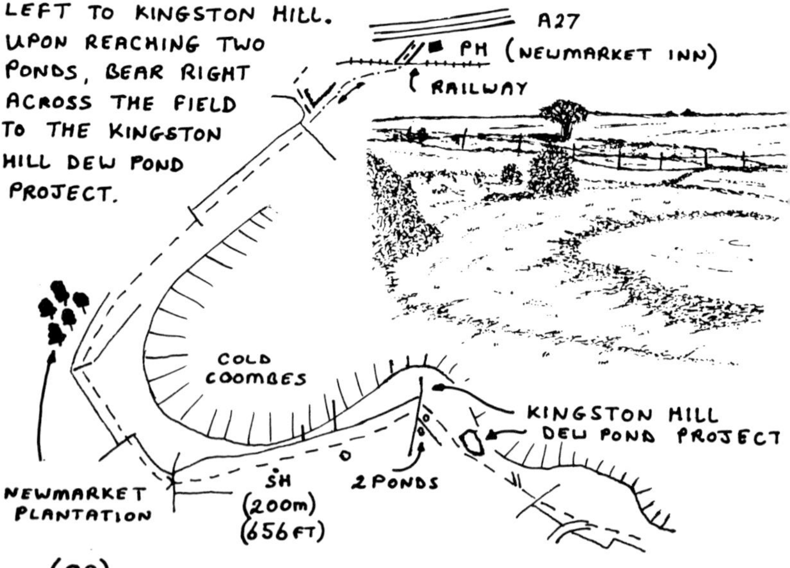

FROM THE DEW PONDS, CONTINUE ALONG THE ESCARPMENT PATH TO A CONCRETE TRACK, WHICH IS FOLLOWED IN THE SAME DIRECTION.

A NUMBER OF DEW PONDS AND TUMULI ARE PASSED EN-ROUTE, SOME MAY EVEN BE SEEN IF THE HEIGHT OF CROPS ALLOWS.

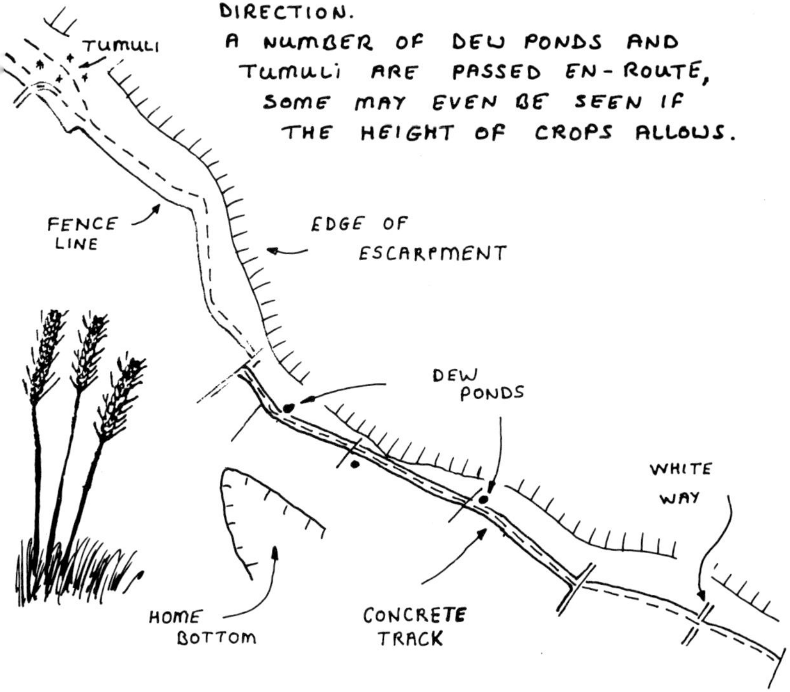

LOOKING N.E. FROM COLD COOMBES AND THE NEWMARKET PLANTATION TOWARDS KINGSTON.

THE S.D.W. EMERGES, VIA A TREE AND HEDGE LINED PATH AT THE TOP OF MILL LANE.
CROSS MILL LANE AND DESCEND, STEEPLY, CRICKETING BOTTOM, WHERE A TRACK TO THE LEFT IS TAKEN.
UPON REACHING SOME FENCING ON THE RIGHT, A SHARP RIGHT TURN IS MADE UP THE HILL.
A LINE OF POSTS MARKS THE WAY TO A GATE AND ROAD JUNCTION.
TURN LEFT, THEN RIGHT. THEN LEFT AGAIN FOR SOUTHEASE.

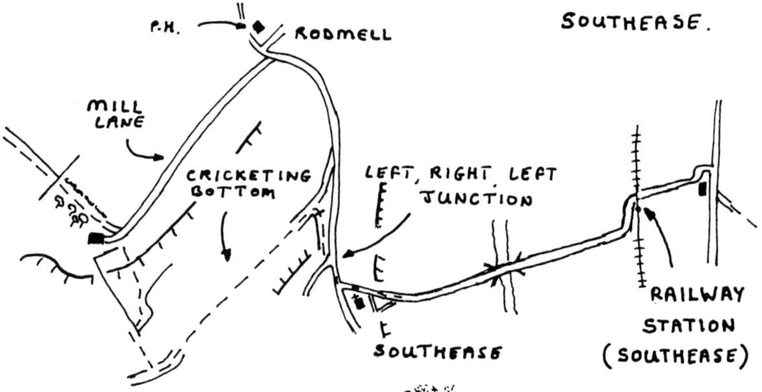

SOUTHEASE CHURCH

RODMELL AND SOUTHEASE.

THE VIEW OF THE LONG WINDING CRICKETING BOTTOM FROM THE SOUTH DOWNS WAY.

ORIGINALLY THE S.D.W. FOLLOWED THE ROAD FROM RODMELL TO SOUTHEASE, AND THIS CAN STILL BE WALKED. HOWEVER A NUMBER OF FAR MORE IMAGINATIVE AND PLEASANT ROUTES CAN BE TAKEN ALONG THE RIVER BANK.

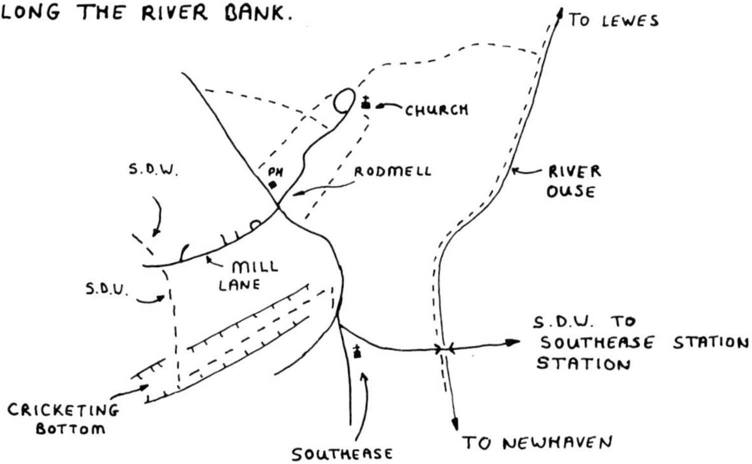

A SIMPLIFIED FOOTPATH MAP OF THE RIVER OUSE, RODMELL AND SOUTHEASE AREA.

SOUTHEASE CHURCH

WHETHER BY TRIAL AND ERROR OR CAREFUL PLANNING, THE VILLAGE OF SOUTHEASE IS JUST ABOVE THE 5 METRE CONTOUR AND THEREBY ESCAPES THE FLOOD PLAIN OF THE RIVER OUSE.
THIS GEOGRAPHICALLY WISE MOVE HAS MEANT THAT A HAMLET HAS SURVIVED FOR MANY CENTURIES.
THE CHURCH IS OF SAXON ORIGIN, AS A BRIEF LOOK AT THE ROUND TOWER WOULD SUGGEST. HOWEVER THE PRESENT STRUCTURE IS OF NORMAN BUILD.

RODMELL

ALTHOUGH NOW BY-PASSED BY THE S.D.W. RODMELL IS A GOOD STOPPING POINT AS A NUMBER OF B&B'S, PUB AND SHOP CAN BE FOUND.

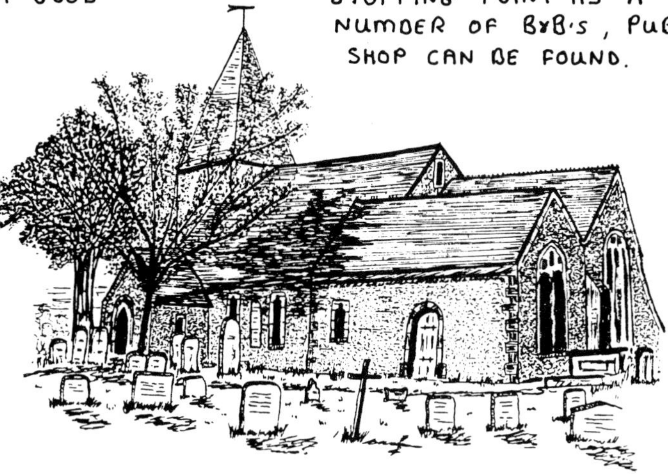

A WALK AROUND THE VILLAGE REVEALS THATCHED COTTAGES, A CHURCH, SCHOOL, THE NATIONAL TRUST OWNED MONKS HOUSE, AND VIEWS OVER THE RIVER OUSE.

THE NORMAN CHURCH AT RODMELL

SOUTHEASE TO ALFRISTON 8m 12km

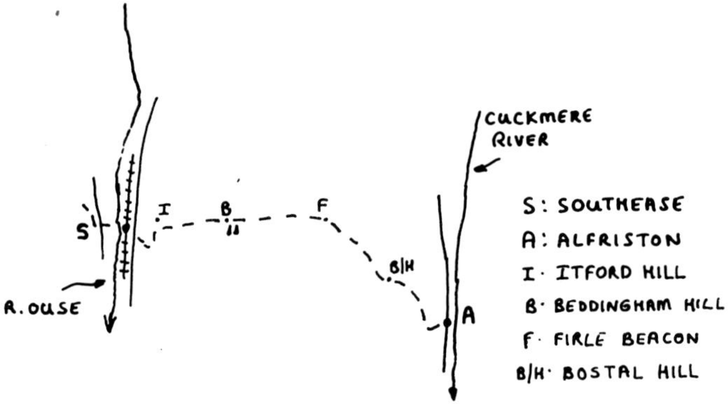

AFTER A CLIMB ON TO ITFORD HILL, FROM SOUTHEAS AND THE RIVER OUSE VALLEY, A GENTLE UNDULATING RIDGE WALK WITH OPEN VIEWS IN ALL DIRECTIONS AWAITS.
THE RED LION POND, BEDDINGHAM HILL, FIRLE BEACON AND BOSTAL HILL ARE NAMED VIEW POINTS BUT EVERY STEP PROVIDES ANOTHER.
ALFRISTON AND THE CUCKMERE VALLEY CAN BE BUS WITH TOURISTS, AND ITS NOT DIFFICULT TO SEE WH WITH THE RIVER, ATTRACTIONS, TEA SHOPS ETC.
THE RELATIVELY SHORT DISTANCE OF THIS SECTION, AND EARLY ARRIVAL TIME IN ALFRISTON OFFERS A TEMPTING WAY OF EXPERIENCING THE BEST OF BOTH WORLDS OF THE FINAL SECTION.
AN EXPLANATION:
IF YOU ARE INTENDING TO WALK THE INLAND ROUT TO EASTBOURNE, THE TIME LEFT TODAY WOULD ALLOW FOR A BUS RIDE TO THE CUCKMERE HAVEN WITH A WALK TO THE COAST TO PHOTO THE SEVEN SISTERS. CONVERSELY...... IF TOMORROW IS TO BE THE COAST ROUTE, THEN A WALK ON TO WINDOVER HILL AND BACK VIA WILMINGTON, WITH VIEWS OF THE LONG MAN IS RECOMMENDED.

FROM SOUTHEASE CHURCH, FOLLOW THE LANE AND CROSS THE RIVER OUSE VALLEY.

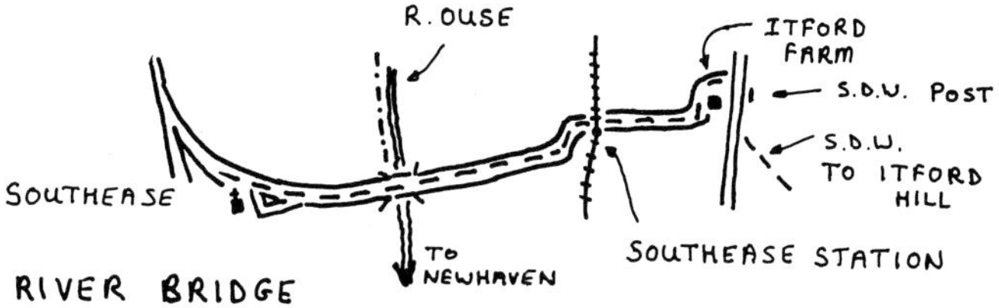

HE RIVER BRIDGE S THE RE-JOINING 'OINT FOR RIVER BANK JALKERS FROM RODMELL.

'TFORD HILL IS IN THE BACKGROUND.

CROSS THE LINE CAREFULLY AT SOUTHEASE STATION, OR BETTER STILL USE THE FOOTBRIDGE.

LEAVE THE ROAD, BY TURNING LEFT ON TO THE TRACK, AND FOLLOW AS IT CURVES AND CLIMBS ITFORD HILL.

THE RED LION POND AND TRIG POINT

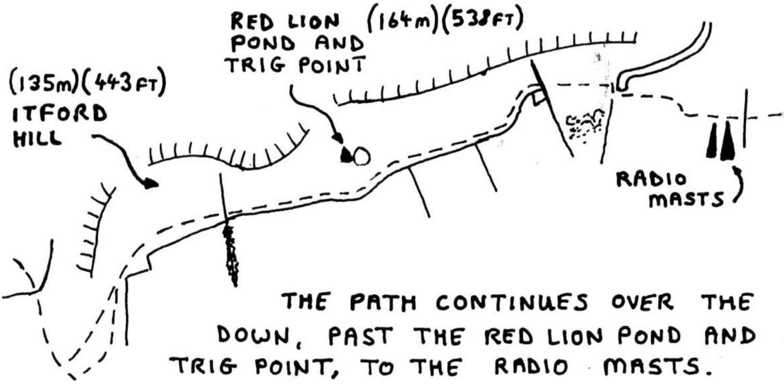

THE PATH CONTINUES OVER THE DOWN, PAST THE RED LION POND AND TRIG POINT, TO THE RADIO MASTS.

LOOKING EAST TOWARD THE BEDDINGHAM HILL RADIO MASTS.

ONTINUE OVER THE DOWN TO THE SMALL CAR PARK
ND ROAD TO WEST FIRLE.
ROSS THE CAR PARK AND FOLLOW THE WELL
EFINED PATH ALONG THE DOWN TO THE TRIG
OINT OF FIRLE BEACON.

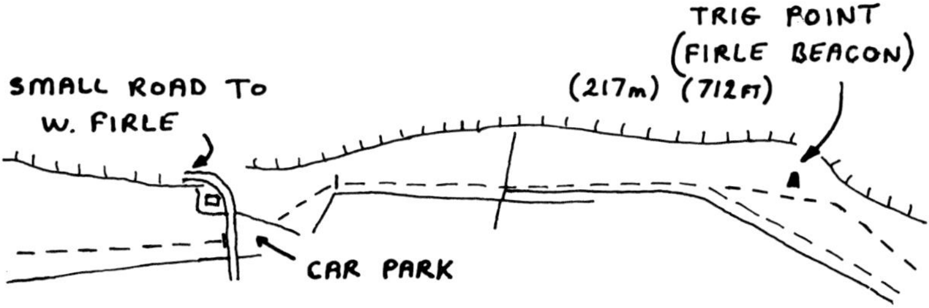

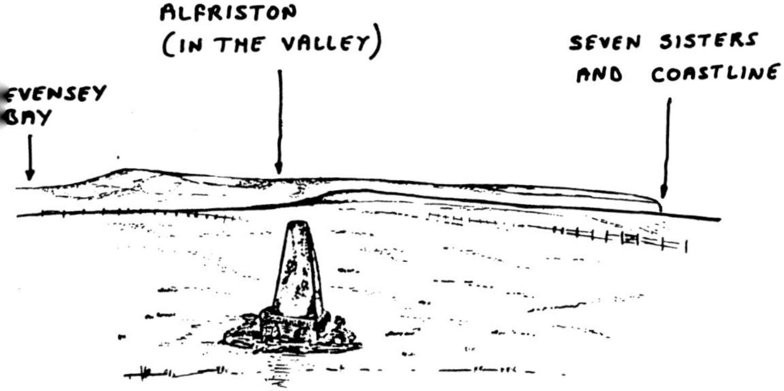

<u>LOOKING SOUTH EAST</u> FROM <u>FIRLE BEACON</u>
TOWARD <u>WINDOVER HILL</u>.

FIRLE BEACON

FROM THE FIRLE BEACON TRIG POINT THE RELIEF OF THE OUSE RIVER VALLEY BECOMES VERY APPARENT. LARGE AREAS OF DOWNLAND AND WEALD HAVE BEEN REMOVED BY WATER AND ICE EROSION LEAVING ISOLATE ISLANDS OF LAND, SUCH AS SAXON DOWN.

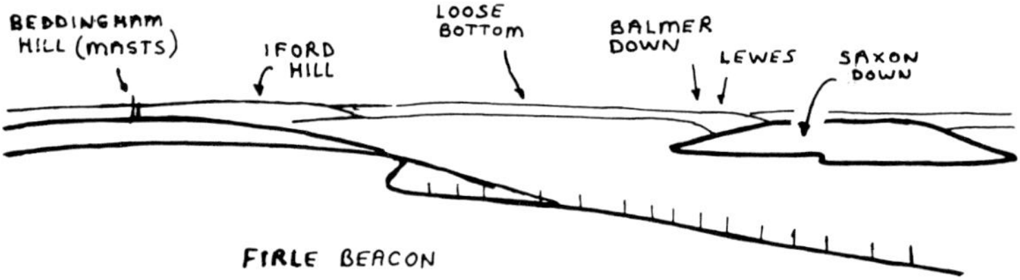

EVIDENCE WOULD SUGGEST THAT THE VALLEY TO THE WEST OF LEWES IS THE REMAINS OF A RIVER THAT ONCE FLOWED EAST TO JOIN THE OUSE AT THE BROOKS. THE RELATIVELY FLAT VALLEY FLOORS HAVE BEEN USED FOR ROADS AND RAILWAYS.

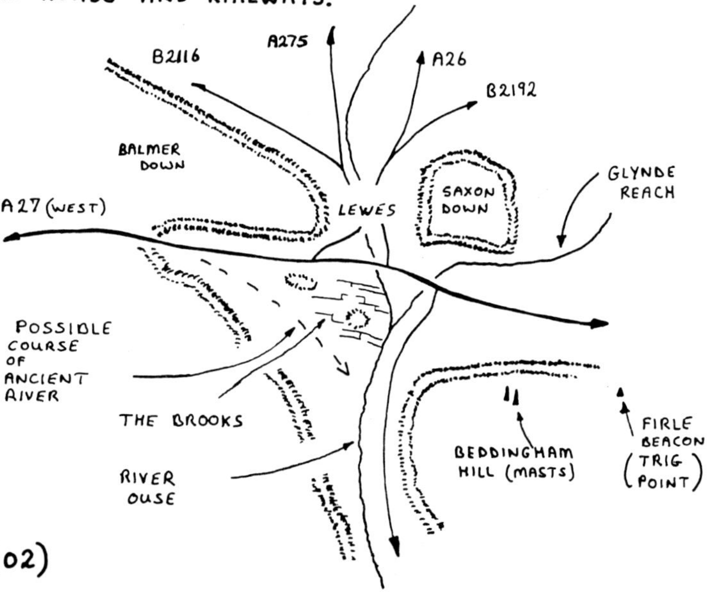

CONTINUE ON THE WELL DEFINED PATH, PAST THE BO PEEP CHALK PIT JUNCTION, AND OVER BOSTAL HILL.

MAINTAIN A SOUTH EAST DIRECTION, AS INSTRUCTED BY THE WHITE POST, UNTIL A SMALL COPSE OF TREES AND THE TRACK DESCENDING TO ALFRISTON.

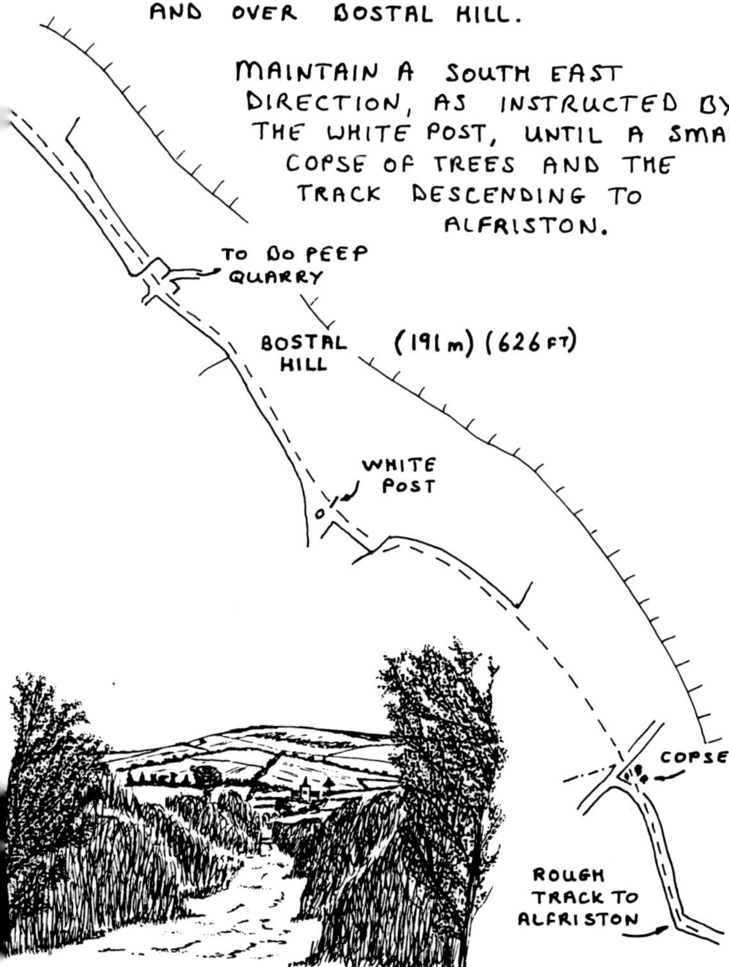

THE APPROACH TO ALFRISTON

ALFRISTON

THE VILLAGE GREEN OR TYE AS IT IS KNOWN LOCALLY GIVES EASY ACCESS TO THE (14) CHURCH OF SAINT ANDREW.

EVERY OTHER CHURCH SEEN SO FAR HAS HAD SOME ADDITION OR REMOVAL OVER THE YEARS HOWEVER, THIS CHURCH BUILT IN 1360, HAS REMAINED UNALTERED SINCE THAT DATE.

THE CHURCH WAS BUILT IN THE SHAPE OF A GREEK CROSS, THAT IS THE TOWER IN THE CENTRE.

THE THATCHED CLERGY HOUSE, ALSO (14) WAS THE FIRST PROPERTY TO BE PURCHASED BY THE NATIONAL TRUST IN 1891.

ALFRISTON

NESTLING IN A TRIANGULATION OF BUILDINGS AT THE NORTHERN END OF THE MAIN STREET IS THE MARKET CROSS.

IT WAS HENRY IV WHO IN 1405 GAVE PERMISSION FOR THE THEN VILLAGE OF ALFRYTON TO HOLD MARKETS.
THE PUBS, SHOPS AND BUILDINGS IN GENERAL ARE STEEPED IN HISTORY.

A WALK THROUGH ALFRISTON IS A WALK THROUGH HISTORY.

LULLINGTON CHURCH

A BRIEF ASCENT OF THE HILLSIDE, TO THE EAST OF ALFRISTON, BRINGS YOU TO THE HAMLET OF LULLINGTON AND THE SMALL CHURCH.

WHAT IS LEFT NOW IS THE CHANCEL OF, WHAT WAS, A BIGGER CHURCH.

A CROP PATTERN SEEN IN THE FIELDS TO THE EAST OF ALFRISTON. 1995.

ORIGINALLY DATING FROM THE 13TH CENTURY, THE SEATED CONGREGATION NUMBERED 20.

SOME OUTLINE WALLS AND FOUNDATIONS CAN STILL BE SEEN AROUND THE BUILDING, IN WHAT IS A LOVELY LOCATION.

LULLINGTON CHURCH

ALFRISTON

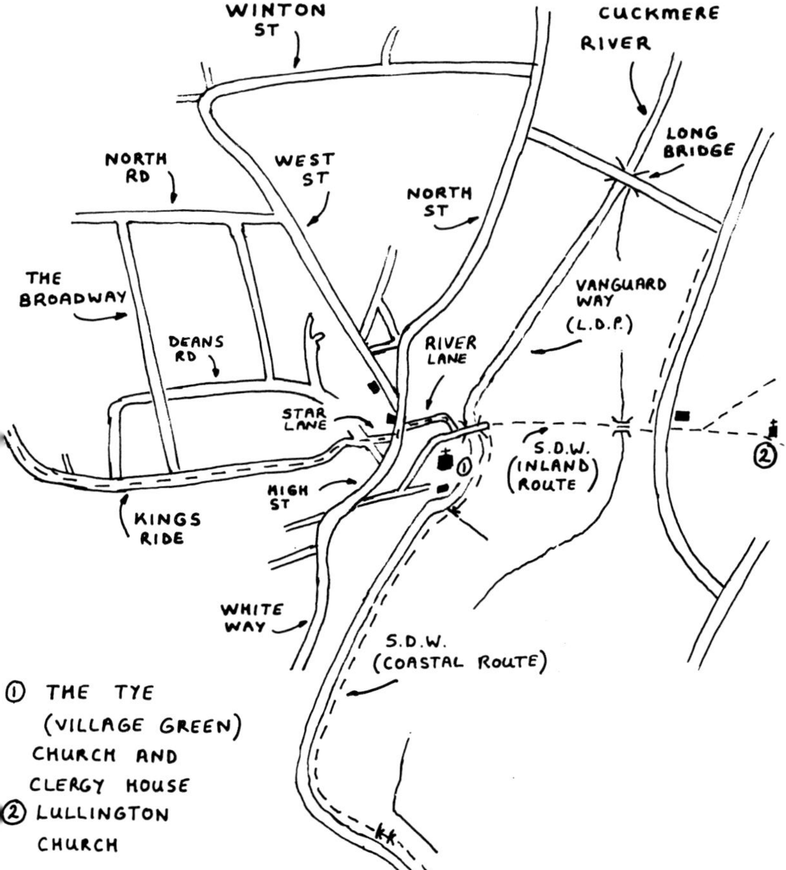

① THE TYE (VILLAGE GREEN) CHURCH AND CLERGY HOUSE

② LULLINGTON CHURCH

VANGUARD WAY

63 MILES (100 Km) OF FOOTPATH FROM CROYDON TO THE SOUTH COAST AT SEAFORD.

ALFRISTON TO EASTBOURNE

COASTAL ROUTE
10½ m 17 Km

INLAND ROUTE
7½ m 12Km

A	ALFRISTON
L	LITLINGTON
E/D	EAST DEAN
B/G	BIRLING GAP
E/B	EASTBOURNE
W	WILMINGTON
J	JEVINGTON
L/M	LONG MAN
C/H	CUCKMERE HAVEN
E/B	EASTBOURNE

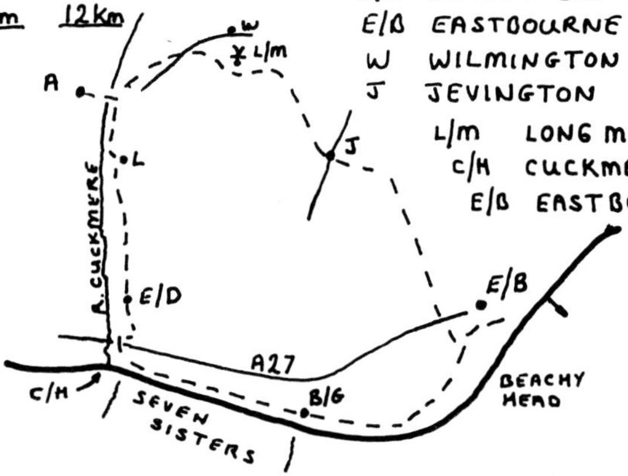

COAST BOUND WALKERS HAVE THE MORE STRENUOUS DAY AHEAD, AND ARGUABLY THE MORE SPECTACULAR ROUTE AND FINISH.
THIS IS NOT TO SAY IT IS BEST AS THE VILLAGE OF JEVINGTON IS VERY PRETTY, AND THE VIEWS FROM WINDOVER AND WILLINGDON HILL ARE PANORAMAS OF 360°..... AND THEY ARE SLIGHTLY HIGHER THAN THE SEVEN SISTERS.
COAST BOUND WALKERS HAVE THE DELIGHTS OF THE CUCKMERE RIVER, THE VILLAGES OF LITLINGTON AND WEST DEAN.
THE UPS AND DOWNS OF THE SEVEN SISTERS, BIRLING GAP, AND THE FINAL CLIMB IS OVER BEACHY HEAD AND ON TO EASTBOURNE.
INLANDERS HAVE WINDOVER HILL WITH VIEWS OF THE LONG MAN AND WILMINGTON FOLLOWED BY JEVINGTON. A SECOND HILL WALK WITH VIEWS ACROSS THE DOWN. AND COAST LEADS TO EASTBOURNE.

THE INLAND ROUTE.

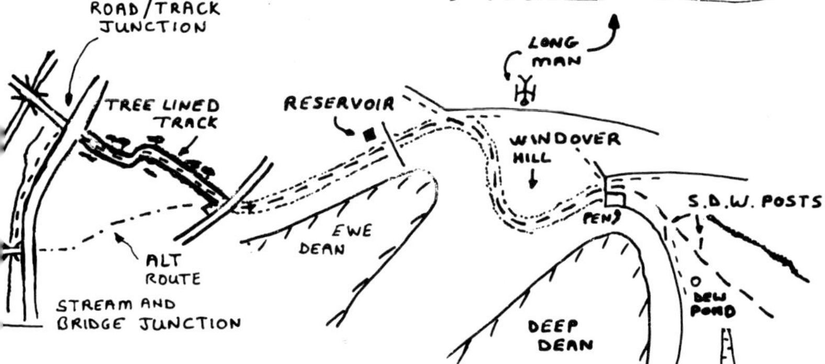

LEAVE ALFRISTON BY THE FOOTBRIDGE OVER THE RIVER CUCKMERE.
UPON REACHING A SMALL STREAM BRIDGE, CROSS AND TURN LEFT THROUGH A FIELD TO THE ROAD AND TRACK JUNCTION.
CROSS THE ROAD IN TO THE TREE LINED TRACK WHICH IS FOLLOWED TO A ROUGH CAR PARK AND LANE.
CROSS OVER THE LANE AND FOLLOW THE WORN TRACK, GENTLY CLIMBING ALONG SIDE EWE DEAN AND THEN CONTOURING AROUND WINDOVER HILL AND DEEP DEAN.

THE STREAM AND BRIDGE JUNCTION TO THE EAST OF ALFRISTON.

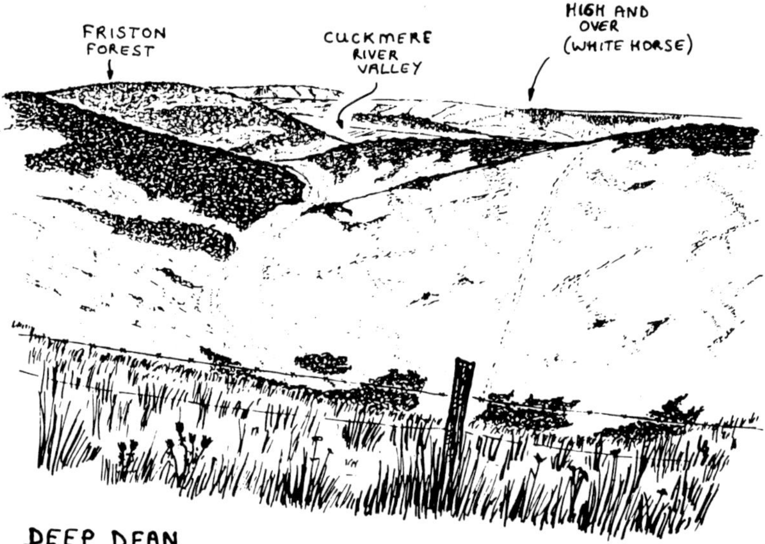

DEEP DEAN

THE S.D.W. PASSES DEEP DEAN AFFORDING VIEWS OF THE VALLEY AND SURROUNDING DOWNS. THE NOT SO DISTANT COASTLINE, CUCKMERE RIVER VALLEY, HIGH AND OVER WITH WHITE HORSE AND FRISTON FOREST.

THE FIRST VIEW OF EASTBOURNE AND PEVENSEY BAY FROM THE S.D.W. ABOVE JEVINGTON HOLT.

LOOKING EAST FROM THE BANKS OF THE RIVER CUCKMERE TOWARD WINDOVER HILL

THE PEACEFUL GROUNDS OF ST ANDREWS CHURCH, JEVINGTON.

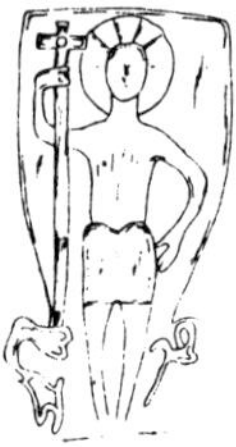

A SAXON SCULPTURE CAN BE FOUND ON THE NORTH WALL.

ST ANDREWS CHURCH AT JEVINGTON.

A SAXON TOWER AND TUDOR WAGGON ROOF ARE WELL WORTH A VISIT

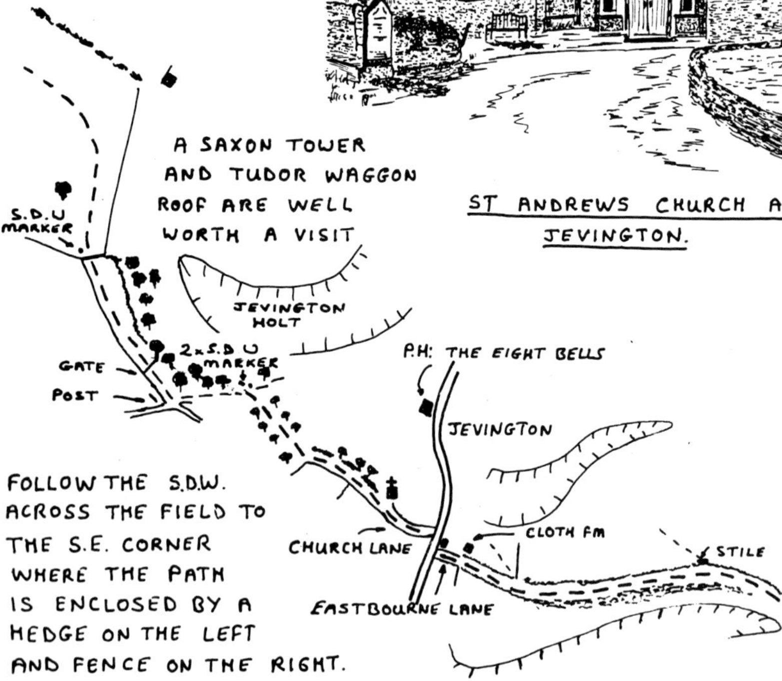

FOLLOW THE S.D.W. ACROSS THE FIELD TO THE S.E. CORNER WHERE THE PATH IS ENCLOSED BY A HEDGE ON THE LEFT AND FENCE ON THE RIGHT.

WATCH FOR THE S.D.W. MARKER POSTS AS A LEFT AND RIGHT TURN LEADS TO CHURCH LANE AND JEVINGTON.

TURN INTO EASTBOURNE LANE AND CLIMB BOURNE HILL.

INLAND ROUTE

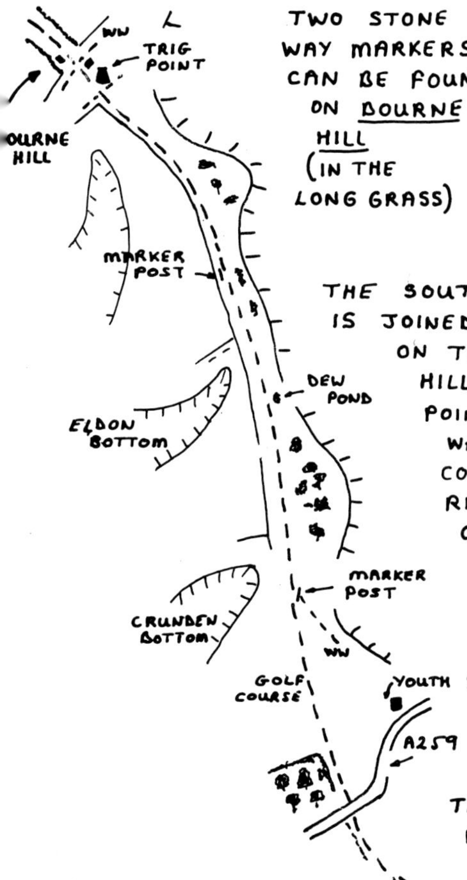

TWO STONE WAY MARKERS CAN BE FOUND ON <u>BOURNE HILL</u> (IN THE LONG GRASS)

THE SOUTH DOWNS WAY (S.D.W) IS JOINED BY THE WEALDWAY (WW) ON THE TOP OF BOURNE HILL, BESIDE THE TRIG POINT AND OLD STONE WAY MARKERS.

CONTINUE ALONG THE RIDGE, PAST THE GOLF COURSE TO THE A259. CROSS THE ROAD.

ONE POSSIBLE FINISH OF THE S.D.W. IS A LEFT TURN, BESIDE THE TRIG POINT, TO PARADISE DRIVE.

THE BEACHY HEAD FINISH IS REACHED BY PASSING TO THE RIGHT OF THE TRIG POINT.

<u>HE DEW POND</u> OFFERS ELCOME SEATS BESIDE HE PARADISE DRIVE PATH

FOLLOW THE PATH AND TREE LINE FOR BEACHY HEAD

COASTAL ROUTE

FOLLOW THE RIVER BANK UNTIL THE GRASS PATH MEETS A TARMAC PATH, JUST BEFORE A SMALL WHITE BRIDGE, WHERE A LEFT TURN IS MADE TO THE VILLAGE OF LITLINGTON. TURN RIGHT, ALONG THE HIGH ST, UNTIL THE VILLAGE HALL IS REACHED. TURN LEFT, AND THEN RIGHT TO CROSS AND CLIMB THE FIELD.

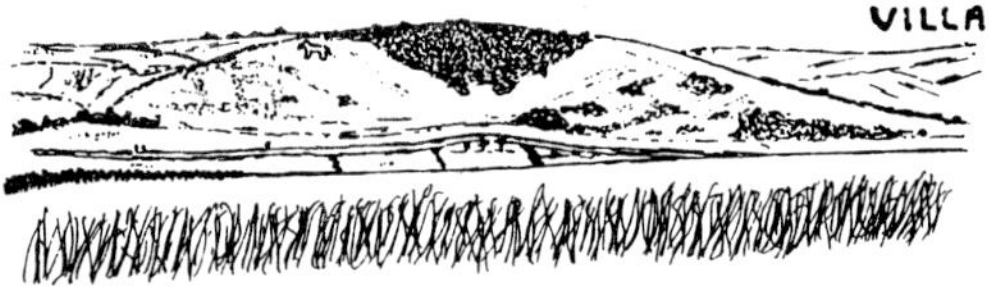

LOOKING WEST TO HIGH AND OVER AND THE WHITE HORSE.

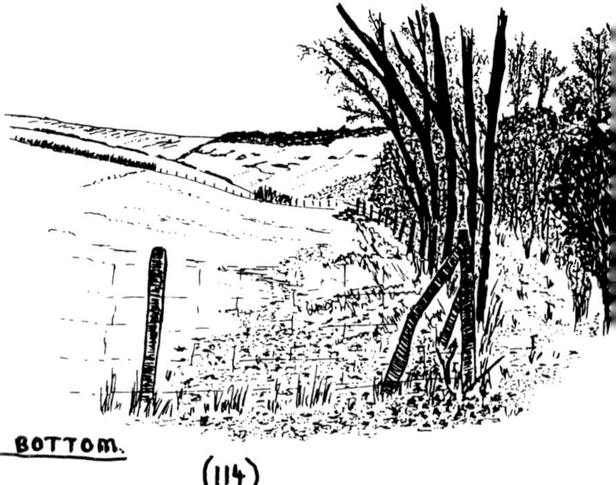

THE S.D.W. LOOKING EAST ALONG CHARLESTON BOTTOM.

LITLINGTON - COASTAL ROUTE

HE FIRST OF TWO DELIGHTFUL VILLAGES ON HIS SECTION OF THE WALK, LITLINGTON IS AN EARLY, BUT WORTH WHILE, STOP.

THE (12) CHURCH OF ST MICHAEL THE ARCHANGEL.

HE CHURCH CAN BE SEEN FROM THE S.D.W. PATH LONG THE CUCKMERE RIVER, HOWEVER FOR A SIT THE ROAD MUST BE FOLLOWED NORTH, BEFORE TURNING TO THE S.D.W.

E LOCAL
UILDING
ONE, FLINT,
AN BE SEEN
MANY OF
HE HOUSES
ND WALLS.
HROUGHOUT
TLINGTON VILLAGE.

COASTAL ROUTE

FROM CHARLESTON BOTTOM, A TREE LINED PATH LEADS TO SOME STEPS, AND UP TO THE TRACK ACROSS FRISTON FOREST. WATCH FOR THE S.D.W MARKER POSTS THROUGH THE FOREST UNTIL A RIGHT TURN AND A STEEP DESCENT TO WEST DEAN.

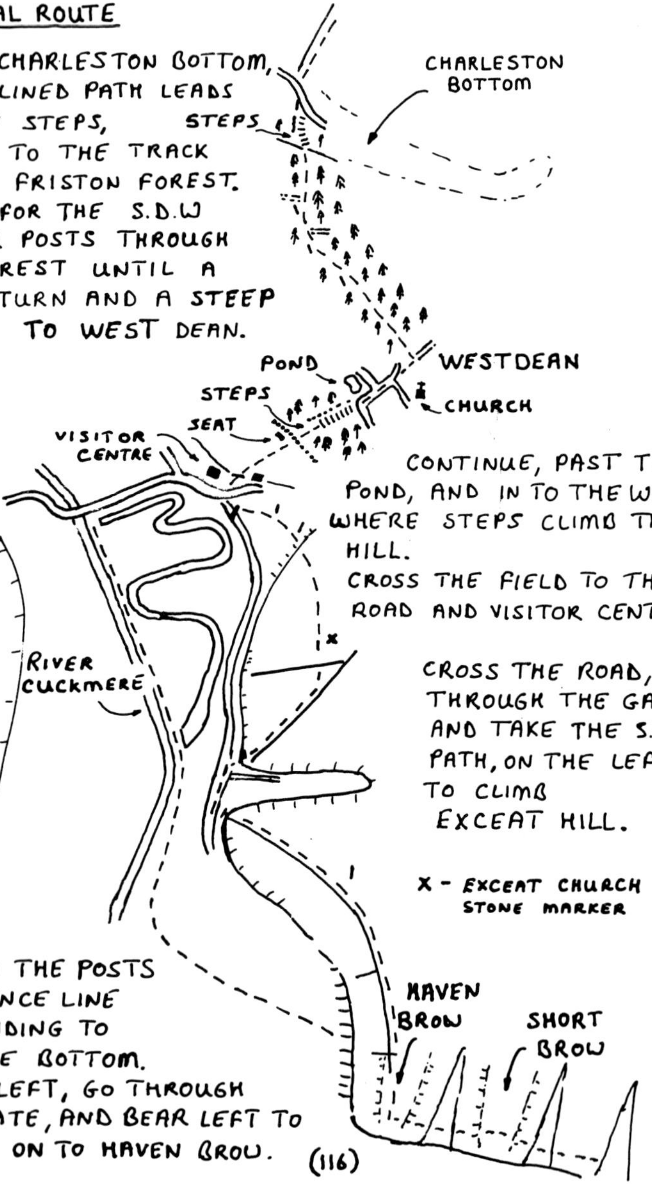

CONTINUE, PAST TH
POND, AND IN TO THE WO
WHERE STEPS CLIMB TH
HILL.
CROSS THE FIELD TO TH
ROAD AND VISITOR CENT

CROSS THE ROAD,
THROUGH THE GA
AND TAKE THE S.
PATH, ON THE LEF
TO CLIMB
EXCEAT HILL.

X - EXCEAT CHURCH STONE MARKER

FOLLOW THE POSTS AND FENCE LINE DESCENDING TO FOXHOLE BOTTOM. TURN LEFT, GO THROUGH THE GATE, AND BEAR LEFT TO CLIMB ON TO HAVEN BROW.

WEST DEAN – COASTAL ROUTE

ALL SAINTS CHURCH. WEST DEAN

EMERGING FROM FRISTON FOREST.....
.. THE FIRST OF MANY WONDERFUL VIEWS OF
CUCKMERE HAVEN.

THE SEVEN SISTERS COUNTRY PARK.

DESCEND FROM FRISTON FOREST AND ITS VIEW POINT AND GEOLOGY BOARD TO THE VISITOR CENTRE AND A FEAST OF DISPLAYS, MAPS AND LEAFLETS AWAIT THE WALKER.
THIS AREA OF DOWNLAND, WOOD, COAST AND RIVER VALLEY IS, QUITE CORRECTLY, BESTOWED WITH MANY TITLES:

AREA OF OUTSTANDING NATURAL BEAUTY.
SITE OF SPECIAL SCIENTIFIC INTEREST.
HERITAGE COAST.
SEVEN SISTERS VOLUNTARY MARINE CONSERVATION - AREA.

IT IS EASY TO SEE HOW A WHOLE DAY CAN BE SPENT HERE AS BIRDS, TREES, PLANTS, SEA-LIFE, GEOGRAPHY, GEOLOGY, SOCIAL AND ECONOMIC DEVELOPMENT ALL FEATURE.
A WALK ALONG THE WESTERN SIDE OF THE RIVER PROVIDES THE POST CARD VIEW OF THE SEVEN SISTER
NB. RIVER CAN NOT BE CROSSED AT MOUTH.

THE CUCKMERE RIVER VALLEY VIEWED FROM THE VISITOR CENTRE.

THE S.D.W. CLIMBS EXCEAT HILL, TO THE LEFT, (EAST). HOWEVER THE CONCRETE ROAD CAN BE FOLLOWED RE-JOINING THE S.D.W AT FOXHOLE BOTTOM.

EXCEAT CHURCH (THE SITE OF)

AN EASILY MISSED STONE MARKER ON EXCEAT HILL READS: FORMERLY STOOD THE PARISH CHURCH OF EXCEAT, PROBABLY BUILT IN XI TH CENTURY AND ABANDONED IN XV CENTURY. PARISH BEING INCORPORATED WITH WEST DEAN IN 1528.
REMAINS FOUND BY SUSSEX ARCHEOLOGICAL SOCIETY 1913.

VIEW FROM HAVEN BROW, OVER CUCKMERE HAVEN TO SEAFORD HEAD, SHORT CLIFF AND HOPE BOTTOM.
IT IS FROM SEAFORD HEAD THAT THE CLASSIC VIEW OF THE SEVEN SISTERS IS SEEN.

COASTAL ROUTE

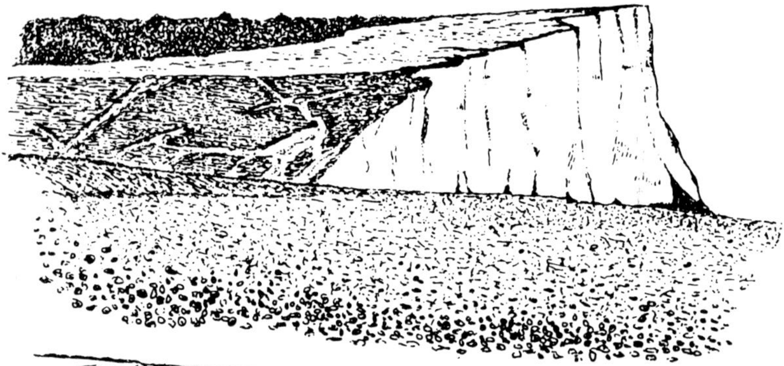

HAVEN BROW FROM THE BEACH

HAVEN BROW AND CUCKMERE HAVEN FROM SHORT CLIFF.

THE "CLASSIC" VIEW OF THE SEVEN SISTERS, FROM SEAFORD HEAD / HOPE BOTTOM.

HAVING REACHED THE TOP OF HAVEN BROW, TURN LEFT AND FOLLOW THE CLIFF LINE OVER THE SEVEN SISTERS TO BIRLING GAP.

DUE TO THE VOLUME OF VISITORS TO BIRLING GAP, AND THE RESULTING EROSION, THE SURROUNDING GRASS AREAS MAY BE ROPED OFF FOR SEEDING, SO HEED THE ROUTE ALTERATION NOTICES.

THE S.D.W. CONTINUES ALONG THE CLIFF LINE.

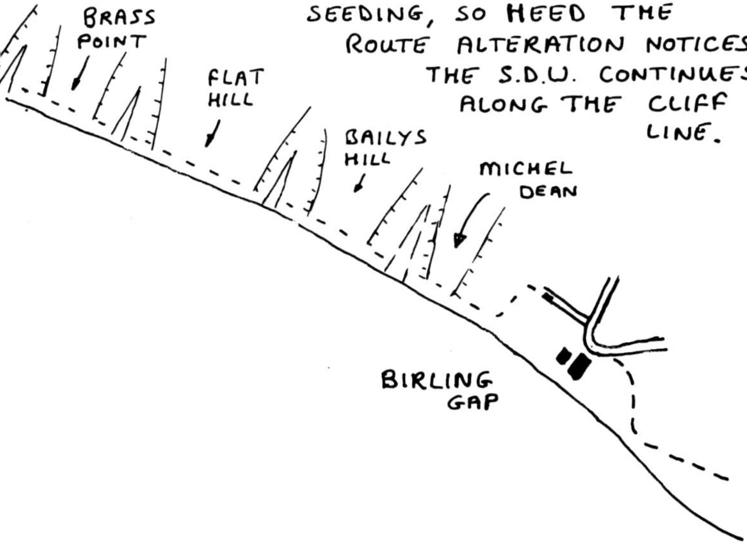

THE SEVEN SISTERS FROM BIRLING GAP.

COASTAL ROUTE

CONTINUE ALONG THE CLIFF LINE TO THE OLD LIGHTHOUSE.
FOLLOW THE PATH, AROUND THE WALL, ON THE LANDWARD SIDE!
CONTINUE WITH THE COAST AS IT DESCENDS TO THE ROAD AND THEN CLIMBS TO BEACHY HEAD.

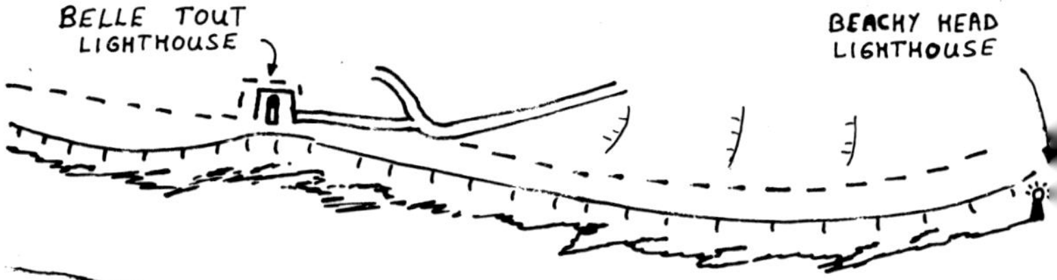

THE BEACHY HEAD LIGHTHOUSE, BUILT IN 1902, AT SEA LEVEL REPLACES THE BELLE TOUT LIGHT HOUSE, BUILT IN 1832 UPON THE CLIFF TOP. THE CLIFF TOP POSITION OFTEN SHROUDED THE LIGHTHOUSE IN FOG RENDERING IT USELESS FOR MARITIME NAVIGATION.

LOOKING WEST TOWARD BIRLING GAP WITH THE BELLE TOUT LIGHTHOUSE ON THE CLIFF TOP.

INLAND AND COASTAL ROUTES COMBINE

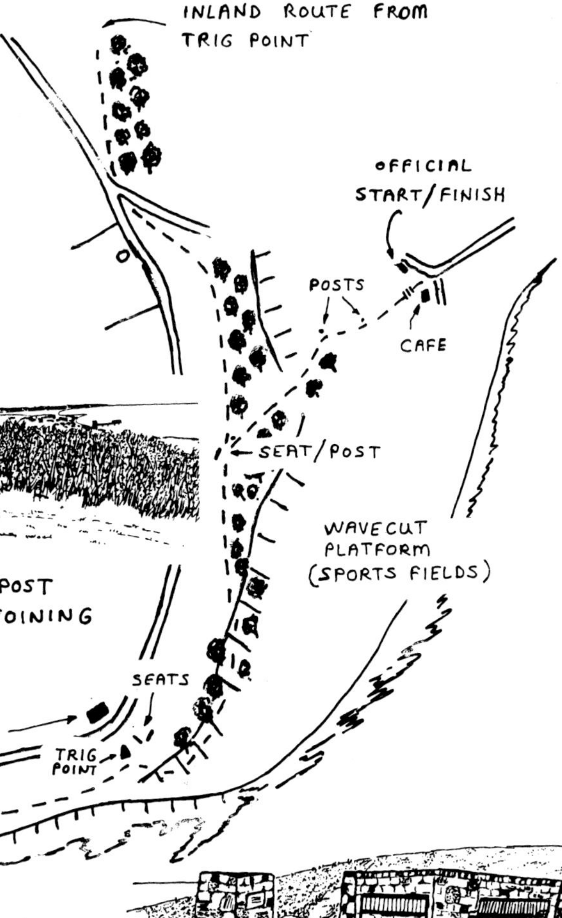

THE SEAT AND POST MARKING THE JOINING OF INLAND AND COAST ROUTES.

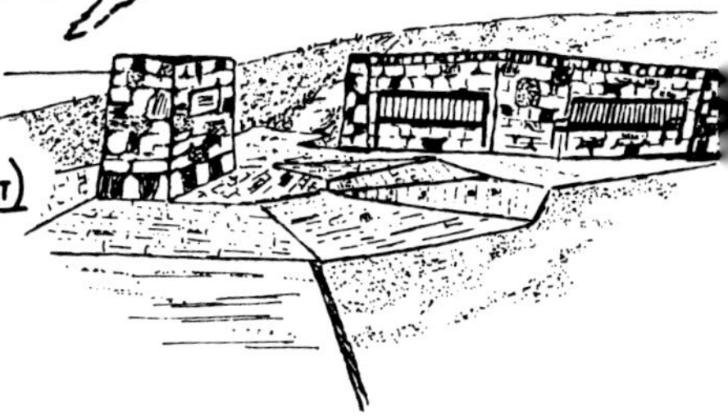

BEACHY HEAD 164m (538FT)

A VISITOR CENTRE, PUB, AND SPLENDID EXTENSIVE VIEWS MAKES BEACHY HEAD A FITTING FINAL HIGH POINT BEFORE DESCENT TO EASTBOURNE

THE FINAL DESCENT TO THE CAFE AND ROAD JUNCTION.

THE EARTHWORKS ARE EASILY MISSED, BESIDE THE HILLSIDE STEPS.

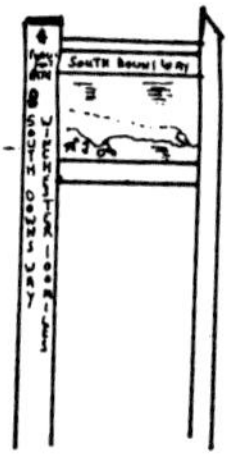

EASTBOURNE

HAVING DESCENDED THE LAST HILL, AND IT IS TRUE, THERE ARE NO MORE HILLS TO CLIMB, THE TEMPTATION IS TO RUSH THROUGH EASTBOURNE IN AN ENTHUSIASTIC FEVER EN ROUTE HOME.
DO NOT MISS OUT ON THIS VERY PLEASANT VICTORIAN SEASIDE TOWN.
IT IS BOTH WISE AND REWARDING TO TAKE A LITTLE TIME TO SAVOUR THE DELIGHTS AS A GOOD SELECTION OF B&BS, RESTAURANTS, PUBS, A SHOPPING CENTRE, PROMENADE AND OF COURSE A PIER, ALL ASSIST IN BRINGING THE SOUTH DOWNS WAY TO A SATISFACTORY AND HAPPY CONCLUSION.

HOLYWELL RETREAT
FROM THE PROMENADE PATH.

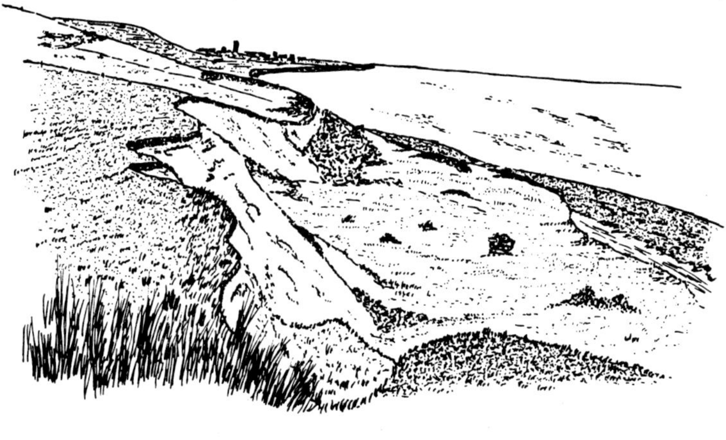

THE OLD WAVE CUT PLATFORM, WITH VIEWS TOWARD EASTBOURNE IN THE NORTH EAST, AND BEACHY HEAD TO THE SOUTH WEST.

EASTBOURNE

THE
WISH TOWER AND LIFEBOAT MUSEUM

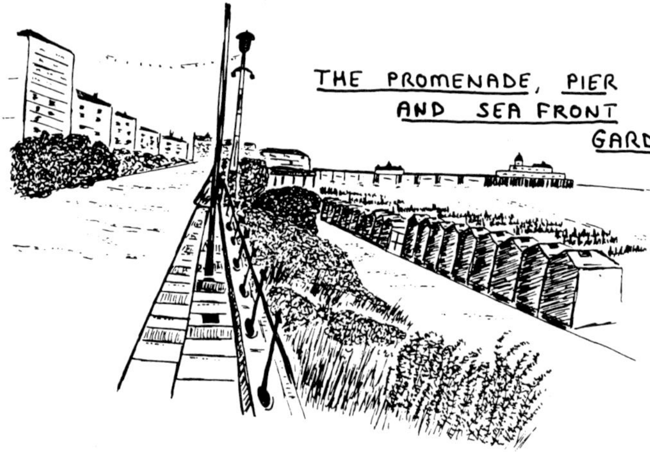

THE PROMENADE, PIER AND SEA FRONT GARDENS.

EASTBOURNE BOASTS SOME OF THE GREATEST NUMBERS OF HOURS OF SUNSHINE EACH YEAR, AND CERTAINLY THE WALK ALONG THE SEA FRONT, PAST THE BEAUTIFULLY MANICURED GARDENS IN SUNSHINE LEAVES ONE IN NO DOUBT.

EASTBOURNE

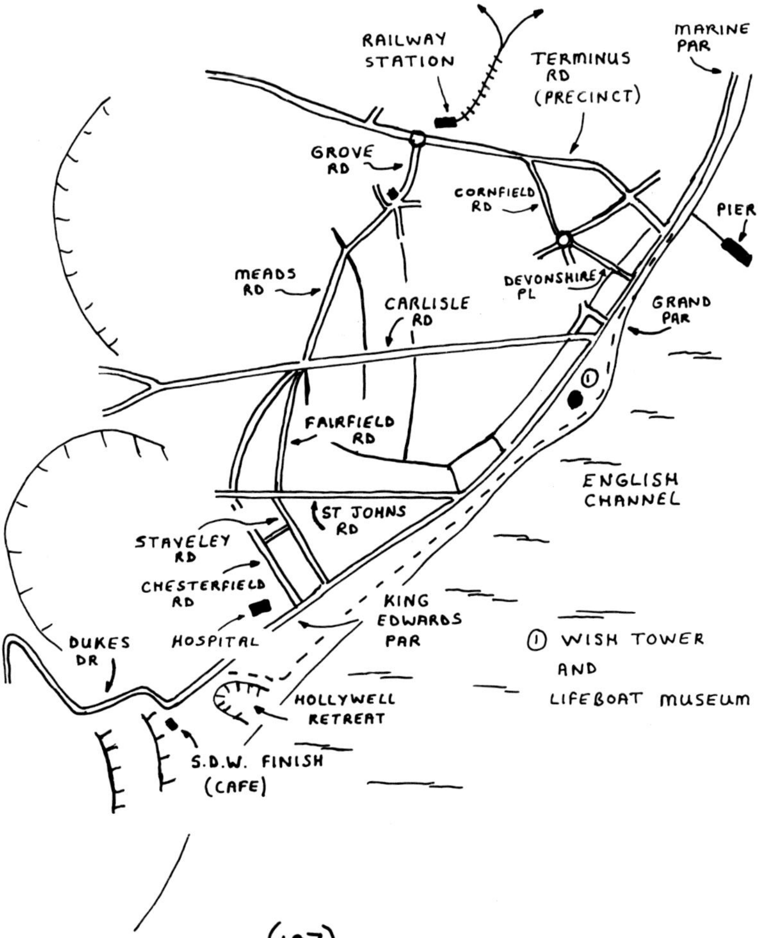
RAILWAY STATION
TERMINUS RD (PRECINCT)
MARINE PAR
GROVE RD
CORNFIELD RD
PIER
MEADS RD
DEVONSHIRE PL
CARLISLE RD
GRAND PAR
FAIRFIELD RD
ENGLISH CHANNEL
ST JOHNS RD
STAVELEY RD
CHESTERFIELD RD
KING EDWARDS PAR
DUKES DR
HOSPITAL
① WISH TOWER AND LIFEBOAT MUSEUM
HOLLYWELL RETREAT
S.D.W. FINISH (CAFE)

THE END

WELL THAT'S IT, OVER 100 MILES OF WONDERFUL HILL WALKING DRAWS TO A CLOSE WITH THE FINAL DESCENT TO EASTBOURNE.

IF THIS PAGE IS BEING READ IN EASTBOURNE HAVING COMPLETED THE WHOLE ROUTE, BEIT IN PARTS OR AS A ONE OFF WALK, THEN CONGRATULATIONS, YOUR EFFORT OF COMPLETING A NATIONAL TRAIL IS TO BE APPLAUDED.

IT HAS TO BE CONCEDED THAT THERE ARE SECTIONS OF SOCIETY THAT WILL NOT UNDERSTAND THE SATISFACTION THAT GOES WITH WALKING FROM WINCHESTER ALL THE WAY TO EASTBOURNE.
SOME MAY EVEN OFFER REMARKS AS... WHAT FOR? OR, I WOULD HAVE GIVEN YOU THE BUS FARE!
YOU KNOW THE INWARD FEELING OF PLEASURE THAT ACCOMPANIES THIS ACHIEVEMENT.

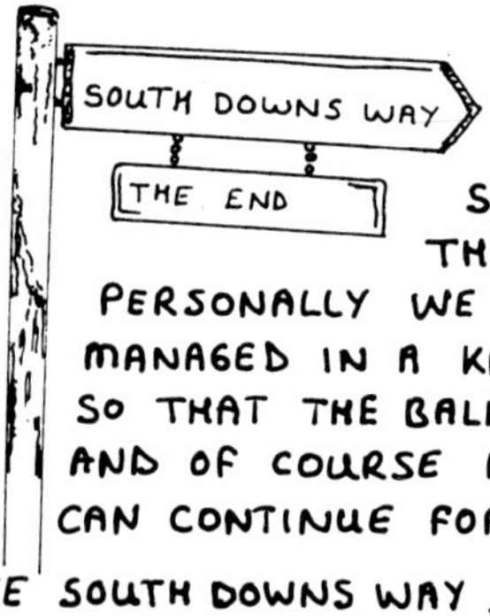

MEMORIES OF HILL TOPS, WOODLAND PATHS, SECLUDED STREAMS AND MILES OF VIEWS, THAT'S THE SOUTH DOWNS WAY.

PERSONALLY WE HOPE THAT THE DOWNS WILL BE MANAGED IN A KNOWLEDGEABLE AND WISE MANNER SO THAT THE BALANCE WITH WALKERS, LANDOWNERS, AND OF COURSE NATURES DELICATE ECO SYSTEMS CAN CONTINUE FOR MANY YEARS TO COME.

THE SOUTH DOWNS WAY ..... A WEEK WELL SPENT.